THE
WHITTAKER
CHAMBERS
READER

His Complete
National Review
Writings, 1957-1959

To obtain additional or bulk copies of
this collection please contact:

National Review
Re: The Whittaker Chambers Reader
215 Lexington Avenue, 11th Floor
New York, NY 10016

ISBN 978-0-9847650-1-0

Please visit our website at
www.nationalreview.com

National Review thanks Kathryn Murdock, Lucy Zepeda,
Catherine Napier, Katherine Connell, Emily Gray, Kim
McCarthy, Matthew Raymond, Nat Brown, and Luba
Myts for the many duties they performed to help bring this
book to fruition.

PRINTED IN THE UNITED STATES OF AMERICA

FOREWORD

C aught up as we are in the daily policy battles that America faces in Washington and state capitals, or in handicapping looming elections, or in the international struggles that threaten our nation and our allies, we conservatives need to find time to remind ourselves that we are just that, conservatives.

It is worthwhile and even inspiring that, on regular occasion, we stop to reflect on our movement, on our beliefs, and on those individuals who have proven fundamental and vital to such—to the people who shaped us, directly or indirectly, to embrace the virtues of small government, personal and economic liberty, free trade, and Pax Americana, and to oppose the aggrandized state, political correctness, the intolerant Left of the academy, and a timid America.

Our founder was a great man—William F. Buckley Jr. And the man Bill thought was great, because he indeed was great, was Whittaker Chambers, who toiled here at *National Review*, albeit too briefly, in the late 1950s.

Chambers was a hero to the fledgling politcal Right, and to foes of communism and fascism and tyranny. His epic public battle against Alger Hiss (and the Communist spy's Establishment and media supporters), along with his powerful memoir, *Witness*—which remains one of the greatest autobiographies ever written—made him a key figure in the founding of the conservative movement.

And a key figure in American history too.

Neither positions which he would have sought, or embraced. But facts are stubborn things, and even Chambers, in his yearning for peace and his disdain for the eye of the storm, could not deny his role.

We stand on the shoulders of giants, so it is said, and if that is true of any institution, it is true of *National Review*. Buckley (Bill and Priscilla), Chambers, Burnham, Bozell, Kendall, Meyer, Rusher were great men and women indeed.

They deserve to be remembered, and with this volume, slim though it is, we remember Chambers. Would our founder have approved? Surely: with a little less than worship, a thing he would reserve strictly for the Almighty, but Bill loved Chambers—as a writer, as a thinker, and as a friend and his pride in Chambers having been part of *National Review* in its early years has filtered down through the decades.

It's been over half a century since his work appeared in our pages, and our offices are different from the magazine's storied early years, but the clutter and debris that were once housed our offices on East 35th Street in New York have somehow followed us to our more recent digs, and some of us Old Timers find it inspiring to know that the typewriter table over there or the bound volumes over here were things once used by Chambers.

He did not write a vast amount for *National Review*: He was an ill man in his last years, plagued by heart ailments that eventually felled him at the age of 60, and had forced him from writing for the magazine two years prior. But what he did write was engaging, insightful, mature, and even notorious—his famous and devastating review of Ayn Rand's *Atlas Shrugged* remains a classic.

This volume is a complete collection of what Whittaker Chambers wrote for *National Review*. We are happy to publish it, to share it, with our compliments, to encourage you to leaf through these pages, to enjoy tremendous writing, and to even find inspiration—to read *Witness* (even if again), and to consider introducing a young person to this man, this Whittaker Chambers, and to explain why his profound witness to history was so important to our movement and to the eventual freedom of hundreds of millions of people.

Jack Fowler
Publisher, *National Review*
October 2014

TABLE OF CONTENTS

SECTION ONE
ORIGINAL WRITINGS

October 26, 1957
Soviet Strategy in the Middle East 1

November 2, 1957
The Coming Struggle for Outer Space 14

November 16, 1957
The Left Understands the Left 19

November 23, 1957
"To Temporize Is Death" 24

December 28, 1957
Big Sister Is Watching You 32

May 31, 1958
Springhead to Springhead 40

September 27, 1958
Some Untimely Jottings 49

October 11, 1958
R.I.P. Virginia Freedom 52

November 8, 1958
A Reminder 54

November 22, 1958
A Republican Looks at His Vote 58

January 31, 1959
Some Westminster Notes 61

February 28, 1959
Missiles, Brain and Mind 64

May 9, 1959
The Hissiad: A Correction 72

June 20, 1959
Foot in the Door 78

SECTION TWO
REMEMBERING CHAMBERS
National Review
July 29, 1961

Letter to William F. Buckley Jr.
Il Faut le Supposer Heureux 87

Duncan Norton-Taylor
Wisdom Is the Most Terrible Ordeal 90

Whittaker Chambers
From a Letter, December, 1959 94

Ralph De Toledano
Let Only a Few Speak for Him 95

Richmond New Leader
Death Deceived 102

October 26, 1957

Soviet Strategies in the Middle East

The bold and imaginative Middle East strategy of Communism should not be underrated, says the author; it implies "the beginning of a direct assault on the United States"

W*estminster, Md.*—Talk, here in the farmlands, is chiefly of the heaviest frost of this date in a decade, and what it may have done to stands of late corn. Yet it cannot be said that we are wholly out of touch with the capitals of the mysterious East—Cairo, Damascus, Baghdad, New York. Thus, a friend, a state legislator, dropped by, a month or so ago, to discuss a matter that was plainly burning a hole in one of the multiple pockets of his mind. Another legislator (from a Western state) had dreamed up a see-it-yourself plan. Paying their own way, a group of lawmakers from all over the country would, one day soon, step into a plane at Idlewild, and, hours later, put down in turn at Cairo, Tel Aviv, Damascus, Baghdad; then, veering north, and again east, at Belgrade and Moscow. Back to the West, if I remember rightly, by way of Warsaw. Everywhere, they hoped to see what eyes can see. In the capitals, they would talk with the makers and shakers. Should he go along? my friend asked.

Looking for the question behind the question, I took it to be: Was there any exceptional danger involved; did I think he could get in and out of the enemy compounds, Cairo, Damascus, Moscow, with a whole skin? Of course, I thought my friend should go along. I thought, too, in passing, that he was his own version of the American dream. Fifty years ago, he had been a farm boy in these same cornlands, hauling his father's crops to market in a horsedrawn wagon. Now, by hard work, and the exercise of a shrewd functional intelligence, he was a man of affairs, entitled to race the speed of sound through space to bespeak other men of affairs in lands far away, though not, unhappily, far enough away. "And what advice will you give Nikita (Khrushchev)?" I asked. The pre-autumn stillness blotted up his laugh.

Age of the Eye-Witness
If I urged my friend to go along, it is not because I set any great store by such excursions, but because others do. Henceforth, this trip would be among my friend's credentials. This is the age of the eyewitness and the first-personer: "I Watched the End of the World." The editor of the *Saturday Evening Post* once told me that it made a difference of thousands of readers if an article carried a title, beginning with the magic words: "I was" or "I did." I did not doubt it. But I doubted something else. That skepticism had set firm in wartime days, when, as a foreign editor, I read with hair-curling depression the reports of old China hands, observing on the spot, and singing in close harmony, that the Chinese Communists were "agrarian liberals." I knew that the Chinese Communists were not agrarian liberals, that, after Hitler's mop-up of the German Communist Party, they were the No. 2 section of the Communist International. But what right did I have to know it? I was not on the spot. How could I presume to pit my view against the close-up of the man on the scene? So I urged my friend: go.

Yet I remain of the opinion that the peering mind, peering even from a cow pasture, even in the jet age, still commands resources of a kind such as carried Dante once as far as Hell and Heaven. So I have sought to pace my friend in his flight, supposing, even, that though earthbound I had some advantages. For the mind has a way of getting into places to which the scheduled flights have been cancelled without advance notice.

I doubt, for example, that my friend made it into Damascus.

Since he left, something fairly tremendous has happened in the Middle East, turning around Damascus as a hurricane turns on its eye. Last night, there appeared on the TV screen the face of the Arab King, Ibn Saud, the Ali Baba of the oil pools, and Washington's late, greatly salaamed guest. A most thought-provoking mask it was at this turn of events, tempting us to say of the man behind it—as Bismarck said of Napoleon III: "A sphinx without a secret." Yet the big Hollywood dark-glasses, vacuous under the Arab headgear, were belied by the royal smile, playing finely on the lips of the long lower face.

The Syrian Upset

King Saud's face was there because he had just left the conference at Damascus, where it had been decided that Syria's Leftist government, Communist inspired, moneyed, munitioned (though largely, it would seem, Socialist-manned) poses no threat to Syria's Arab neighbors. In short, all the Washington blandishments had failed, as yet, to detach this king-pin completely, or really to dent the Arab front. I waited for the commentator to say: Something pretty tremendous has happened. But the press does not editorialize all the news at once, and where it feels least sure of itself is most likely to "report objectively." Last night, we were editorializing the woes of James Hoffa and Little Rock—cleverly, too; that is, not openly, but by selective emphasis. About Syria and Ibn Saud we got the news unchewed.

For once, this seemed a pity. In the sum of things, Hoffa and even Little Rock are comparatively pipsqueak. It is Syria that touches home. It is a great upset—not necessarily irreversible, or in the grand style, but sufficient unto Communism's strategy of the hour. It means that, at its second important test of containing Communism, the Eisenhower Doctrine has contained chiefly a mirage. It means that the Comrade has taken his longest stride across the Western encirclement, and squats outside it, smiling effacively, from a Mediterranean lodgement, with the condoning

Arab lands spread out beyond, inviting mischief.

> *Picture the lewd delight,*
> *Under the bridge tonight.*

Any bridge, that is, across the Moskva River.

A Revolutionary Icebreaker

Whose is the fault? Not the Administration's, I think. Certainly not Mr. Dulles', though he is always the handy whipping-boy, never more so than for those who shout loudly that something has gone wrong while sighing with covert relief when such mischance also means that another crisis will abate. Possibly, with the Arab sanction, this particular Syrian crisis will abate, however bumpingly, because we are flummoxed, because Communism has gained its position, and, for the moment, does not need to push so hard; needs, in fact, a breathing-spell for consolidation and the next advance, which will mount the next crisis. How can it be otherwise, given the Middle East? Before the British-French-Israeli descent on Egypt, I wrote to the editor of this magazine—differing sharply, as I sometimes do, with its reading of events—somewhat like this: "The great hook, which Communism has contrived for us in the Middle East, is that no matter what we do will be wrong. If we back Britain against Egypt [Nasser had seized the Suez Canal], we rally Arab Asia and Africa against us. If we let Nasser get away with it, Communism gets away with it. Yet, on the whole, it seems to me that, of two bad alternatives, Dulles has chosen the slightly better one."

It is necessary to try to grasp 1) what Communist Middle East strategy implies over-all, and 2) how heavily the basic situation there is weighted against us. After the Egyptian dustup, that strategy was interrupted for a time, not only, or perhaps even chiefly, by the stiffness of the American challenge to it, or the commotion in the Soviet satellites. Hesitation in the Middle East more probably reflected resistance in Moscow, on the part of a faction that we call (loosely) Stalinist. What ensued was a new crest of what we call (even more loosely) "the power struggle in the Kremlin." That power struggle must have taken the form, in part, of a ferocious debate over Middle East strategy. And matters must have been immensely confused when Dmitri Shepilov, until then a front runner of that strategy, supposing that he saw the hunt going against him, began to tiptoe to the Stalinist side. As we know, he supposed wrong. The Stalinists lost out, though how completely, or for how long, even Khrushchev may not know much better than we do. But, with that, the Communist Middle East strategy was back with us. We are told that, in the great Kremlin debate, it was described as an "icebreaker" strategy. Of course, the strategy is new only in its specific application in the changed circumstances of 1957— namely, to overleap the military-political encirclement with which the West has ringed Communist aggression as with an icebarrier: to overleap that, and set fire to inflammable nations and continents beyond. In this sense, it is a revolutionary icebreaker.

It is a strategy of great imaginative boldness. It is two-pronged. It strikes (*inter alia*) at 1) the Arab oil pools; it promotes 2) Communism's advance along the North African land-bridge. (How long that takes, using how many false faces, about-faces, how much sinuous indirection—those are tactical problems.) The North African thrust is itself at least two-pronged. One prong aims to soften up Europe in several ways, by pinching the arteries of its oil-fed industry (we saw the threat hang poised during the Egyptian crisis; and in this case it is not true, as Nietzsche said, that "Damocles never danced better than under a sword"). Eventually, the same prong hopes to face Europe with a second front, no farther off than the width of a Mediterranean, no longer "Our Sea," but a sea where we coexist with *them*.

Latin America

The second prong is headed much farther West, toward the

Atlantic gap, where the bulge of Africa approaches the bulge of South America. (Communism loves contiguity and easy overland routes, with the narrowest possible water-jumps.) Most of us do not think much or often about Latin America, except, perhaps, as the cut-rate vacation—land of the colored airline ads. We may be absolutely sure that Moscow thinks a great deal about it, and quite differently. From time to time, we have seen spastic specimens of that thinking, attempting to become deed, in Argentina, Chile, Brazil, Colombia, Guatemala, and (acutely at the moment) in British Guiana. We may also be sure that what Moscow sees looks something like this: a continental human mass, where the solvent community is stretched, taut and thin as a polyethylene film, over impoverished millions who barely manage to subsist at a level of backward misery all but unimaginable to us, in the land of: "Just add hot water and serve." In the Western hemisphere, Latin America reproduces, with its own variants, most of the social inflammabilities of Asia. Latin America is Asia in our own backyard. It is this lode of social cordite that Communism's trans-African prong has in view. No doubt we are tired of hearing that the road to Paris runs through Peking. The road to Washington runs through Rio de Janeiro and Mexico City. But first it runs through Damascus, Cairo and Algiers. It is the prospective path along which travels a little fuse, a mere sputter yet, toward the high explosives of the Western world. In this sense, Communist Middle East strategy implies the beginning of a direct assault on the United States.

But a strategic concept is still far from a strategic reality? And Russians are not ten feet tall? Forty years ago, most of Communism was a handful of seedy outlaws, piling their plates with cigarette stubs during endless wrangles in the Swiss equivalent of beaneries. But they were wrangling in terms of the world. They now control a third of it, and even (since I began writing this) overlook the rest from space, from that mechanical moon whose circlings must be seen as the latest outcome of those circling Swiss wrangles. I beg you, do not underrate the energy of the Communist will or the sweep of its strategic vision, simply because it seems improbable to you.

The Sin Against Reality

If for no other reason, the need to pinch that Communist fuse close to the quick, and at a stroke, justified the Eisenhower Doctrine, all its risks and inadequacies at once conceded. The same need justified the repudiation of our old friends, Britain and France, during their Egyptian descent. And that, quite apart from the high moral phrases—no doubt devoutly believed in by the phrasers—which helped to transfigure (and to blur) what was, when cut to the bone, a necessity of raw power; the necessity to block the Communist thrust before it got galloping. Moral turpitude—how bizarre the words sound by Communist contrast, by contrast with the overarching provocation (and its implications) that triggered the Anglo-French act. Against Egypt, moral turpitude was the least of the sins of Britain and France, whose chief sin was the one for which history gives no absolution—the sin against reality. Reality was defined here by a debility of will, enacted in a debility of performance, of those two quondam powers, bled white and exhausted in two world wars and their consequences, so that they could no longer strike, even in concert, with a force which would redeem its risks in the world's one universal coin: success, for they could not act at all without inciting that rally of Asia and Africa against the West, which, in the context of the Communist conflict, was a dated luxury that the West could no longer afford.

We might do worse than glance at the reminder that Mommsen set at the threshold of this age: "History has a Nemesis for every sin: for the will to freedom that fails in force, as well as for the pride of mind that fails in understanding." So the Egyptian crisis disclosed, as its core meaning, chiefly this: that leadership of the West had at last to become one with where real power in the West alone lay—in the United States. This, regardless of what anybody might want or of the quality of leadership.

Historical Imperative

The same need justified our philanderings with Ibn Saud, unseemly to some, preposterous to others. Who else was there to philander with? Mr. Dulles could have had few illusions. It is scarcely three years since King Saud had his finance minister's right hand chopped off (it had made away with some $3 million of the royal oil receipts), and nailed up in a public square of the capital. If this seems an exotic trifle in an age when great European governments, claiming to be civilized, have organized the planned massacre of millions, it is a trifle which stands for much that must be intensely repugnant to Mr. Dulles, who would not willingly see even Mr. Harold Stassen's right hand nailed to a desk in Foggy Bottom. But history gives you certain pieces to work with, and gives no others. It gave Mr. Dulles Ibn Saud.

In the Middle East, we are in the presence of two energies, which, for convenience, we may separate, but which, in fact, interlock. The first of those energies is political revolution, express in Egypt and Syria, smouldering everywhere. It takes the diverse forms of Arab Nationalism. For historical reasons that we all know, it is prevailingly, often fiercely, anti-Western. Yet for a variety of reasons, Arab Nationalism is constrained to work with the West. For a variety of reasons, of which two—our need to pump out Arab oil, and our need to contain Communism—are foremost, the West is constrained to work with Arab Nationalism.

A Spectrum of Sheiks

In doing so, in replacing Britain as the paramount power in the Middle East, and seeking to contain Communism there in the gambles and gambols of power politics, we deal, perforce, with a spectrum of sheiks of varying shapes and sizes. The Kings, Ibn Saud and Hussein of Jordan, may be taken to stand close to one end of that spectrum. Toward the other end, stand the Christian Arab leaders (a rather different breed) of the Lebanon, the main American beachhead. Somewhere in between, stand the Iraquis. Everywhere, the coin we deal in is Arab Nationalism, supplemented (one hopes, at least) by our skill in dispensing much more tangible coin, as we should because we must. It is a game that requires the utmost in tact, steadiness of nerve, and experience, which, as newcomers, we must gain largely by doing. It is a game, too, in which we may expect only partial or impermanent successes (Jordan looks, at the moment, to be one of these).

We are now up, now down; nothing is final; all is in flux. And we are not the only player on the field. At this level, Communism can play the game, too, and adroitly. It has, besides, the advantage of a master piece, which it can use in ways denied to us. Wherever we seek to regroup Arab Nationalism in the interest of the West, Communism advances that disruptive master piece. We all know what it is, though no one likes to mention it. It is the State of Israel. At once, it becomes necessary to define our intentions clearly. A filthy anti-Semitism afflicts many minds in the West. Nothing is gained by denying it. So let us say flatly: in Christendom, no mind can claim to be civilized and, at the same time, be anti-Semitic, any more than an American mind can claim to be civilized and be anti-Negro. For all Christians, regardless of creed, the Vatican has defined the position once for all: "Spiritually, we are Semites." Moreover, an immense compassion—mere good will is too genderless a term—before the spectacle of the Jewish tragedy in our century, must move our hourly understanding of what the State of Israel means in terms of a hope fired by such suffering.

Let us be quite sure that we know this. For it is also necessary to look at Israel in terms of Middle East reality. Communism may lose friendly Egypt or Syria; it will look for purchasable pawns elsewhere. It is Israel, as an enemy, that Communism cannot afford to lose. Israel is Communism's indispensable piece in the

Middle East, so that a firm Israeli Arab settlement would be the greatest disaster that could befall Communism in that region. The crux of the problem is not chiefly, as we so often hear, the question of resettling the Arabs displaced from Palestine. The crux is the Arab fear of Israeli expansion. Communism has only to tweak that nerve of Arab fear, and, at the touch, Arab Nationalism closes ranks, despite our utmost effort, despite the ferocious animosities sometimes dividing the Arab leaders themselves. Thus, at the power-political level, the Middle East situation is weighted against us by this all but unsolvable problem.

Yet Israel is chiefly useful to Communism at that level, and, perhaps, chiefly at this stage. Over the long haul, the Middle East is weighted against us by something much deeper-going. That something is an incipient social revolution whose makings are everywhere. It is the fermenting energies of that revolution that Communism counts on. If we think little about Latin America in such terms, most of us think scarcely at all about the Middle East.

Why Arabs Choose Communism

Imagine a vast region, most of it empty desert, where cities are few, where thousands live in caves, or, at a higher level, in hovels or slums, though these words of ours scarcely convey the Arab reality. Here, an illimitable poverty is the norm, a poverty made sodden by endemic disease, dark by endemic illiteracy and by an absence of hope that may best be called hereditary. Where, among millions, the daily struggle to eat at all is the term in which the possibility of hope first presents itself, hope turns, easily to social revolution. Anything serves to turn it. Arab Nationalism turns it, and cannot anywhere mount its political revolution without at the same time stirring the energies of the social revolt, and blending with them, until political and social revolution tend to become one. At that fusion point is bred the Arab Communist, a comparatively new development. It is on such native shock troops that Communism counts; and, as usual with Communism, it is not numbers, but a certain kind of knowing fanaticism, resolute and resourceful, that matters.

How easy it is for Communism to work with those social revolutionary energies, which it needs only to set in motion in order to win half its battle. How much easier than for the West, which does not want them set in motion, which, in so far as it works with such energies at all, must work to moderate, restrain and channel them toward peaceable development, while helping these destitute populations to reach a level of minimum well-being, which may act as a brake on revolution. That takes time. It also takes capital. It is surprising, is it not? to see revolution turning on a question of capital. Yet so it is in the Middle East. This is, of course, one of the aspects of foreign aid; and those who set themselves most implacably against it, might brood upon this context. For what is needed here are the irrigation ditch, the factory, and the dam that supplies the ditch and powers the factory, and all the enterprise the factory feeds and stands for.

There are only two sources of such capital—the West and the Communist Empire. Presumably, the West has a good deal more capital to invest, or even to expend, than Communism has. But, again, how much easier it is for Communism. Western capital must, in the nature of things, expect a proper return on its loans, both in the form of interest and tangible advantages, chiefly political, which are a justified collateral. But to the Arab of all classes, therefore, the West appears, or can easily be made to appear, as the niggard banker, whose prudent doles serve to replace a political imperialism, of which the memory is green, by an economic imperialism which the Arabs fear is the other side of the political coin.

How different Communism looks. If its imperialism is of an enslaving frightfulness unknown since Rome's, the Arabs have no direct experience of it. If Communism has less than the West to give, it needs to give less; and it can dole out its credits at rates of interest that radically undercut the West. For, with Communism, capital is the exclusive property of the State, which can assign it where it best promotes Communism's political purposes. Nor does Communism need to disperse its bounty to gain its ends. It can spot it for best effect. Easy credits to Egypt or to Syria, and these places become show-windows in the great Middle East bazaar, to which all eyes are drawn. Moreover, these are down-payment on a promise that need not be kept. If the situation develops favorably to Communism, it will not be kept. But if the West interferes with those who accept the Communist bounty, the West appears to be interfering with the promise. No doubt King Saud's action at Damascus was motivated, at least in part, by this realization, and his fear of the effect which our interference might have, in such terms, on Arab minds. For the Communist promise, though largely unfulfilled, is lure enough. And it is cheaper than foreign aid.

Not all, or even a great many, of the Arabs who take Communist cash, can be Communists. But "O, take the cash and let the credit go" is an Eastern admonishment. It is also the impulse of the needy anywhere. The literate Arab, who is not yet a Communist, can have few illusions about what he is doing. He knows that to play with Communism is a dangerous game. He has weighed the risks and discounted them. Meanwhile, he has the credits to buy the guns (yonder lies Israel!), and to finance at least some small beginnings of the irrigation ditch, the dam and the factory.

And the illiterate Arab, in his miserable millions, what does he think? How can anyone know? But there is evidence that a whisper has run through the caves and hovels, as far south as the Sultanate of Oman and Muscat, and the Saudi wastes, that help has come from that great Power in the steppes, where—praise be to Allah!—the workers have seized the factories and the peasants divided the land—or so the prophets have said. Let us remember that it was a Nobel Prize winner of the West, who, after the Communist-planned massacre by famine of some four million peasants, still hailed the Soviet Union as: "That great light in the East." Should we be surprised if a ragged fellah knows no more?

The Moscow Mirage

But have not these wretched Arabs heard, too, that in Soviet Siberia several million of their co-religionists exist in a misery not much different from their own? Possibly they have heard. Radio has put everybody in the next room from everybody else. The air is crisscrossed invisibly at all hours by warning and hectoring voices. Moreover, and particularly in illiterate lands, news of this kind travels with surprising speed, nobody quite knows how. So perhaps they have heard. But "Russia is wide and the Tsar is far away" was a peasant saying even in our boyhoods. It is extremely difficult to imagine a reality other than our own; and, if our own is desperate, the feat becomes almost impossible, and, in addition, pointless. We need not be too surprised, perhaps, if there is vaguely taking form at the back of the eyes that watch from the slums and the deserts, a vision that has little to do with reality, which distance itself has stripped of the monstrous reality—a vision of Moscow as a mythical Tsarigrad, the symbol of present power, credits, but, above all, of hope.

And where are Washington, New York and London? No screening distance has mercy on them. The wretched Arab sees their tokens all about him in shapes financed by oil profits (and others) of the West's necessary allies. He sees them in the dusty flash of a royal Cadillac, steaming past the mud huts, in the $90 million palace which King Saud has conjured up from the unirrigated sands.

This is the picture I see, peering from my cow-pasture. It is stroked in, of necessity, in gross shorthand, with gross omissions and simplifications. All I have meant to do is to suggest certain considerations which, it seems to me, are somewhat overlooked, but which would seem to bear heavily on the outcome of history in the Middle East. I am curious to learn what first-hand impressions my legislative friend brings back from his Eastern travels, to correct my own.

November 2, 1957

The Coming Struggle for Outer Space

TV utilized a break in a Braves-Yankees broadcast to amplify the first, skeptical announcement of a day or so before that Sputnik really was up there. Listening to the somewhat breathless confirmation ("it says: 'Beep! Beep!'") I laughed. Neighbors, who happened to be present, asked why. I could only answer: "I find the end of the world extremely funny." "What's funny about that?" one asked. What could I answer: that men always defy with laughter what they can do absolutely nothing else about? Beyond that, any explanation I attempted would have been as puzzling as my reaction seemed.

I think I should have had to begin something like this. In 1923, I was sitting in a restaurant on the Kurfuerstendamm, in Berlin. What did the mark then stand at—40 million to the dollar? The exact ratio of catastrophe is unimportant. In Germany, inflation had wiped out all small and middle bank accounts, and the value of all wages, pensions, payments, as completely and inexplicably as if the top floor of a skyscraper had collapsed and dropped the whole nation to the ground. Germany, in 1923, was a madhouse of stunned, desperate, tormented millions.

On the sidewalk beyond my table, there walked past a handsomely dressed, extremely dignified woman. It would miss something to say that she was crying. Tears were streaming down her face—tears which she made no effort to conceal, which, in flowing, did not even distort her features. She simply walked slowly past, proudly erect, unconcerned about any spectacle she made. And here is what is nightmarish: nobody paid the slightest attention to her. The catastrophe was universal. Everybody knew what she signified. Nobody had anything left over from his own disaster to notice hers.

She became one of my symbols of history in our time. About this unknown, slowly walking, weeping woman, as about certain other things, no more momentous, that were around me in those days, I came to feel at length as Karl Barth said of something else: "At that moment, I found my hand upon the rope, and the great bell of prophecy began to toll." I began then (along with thousands of others) to draw certain conclusions about the crisis of history in this time that I can merely sketch in like this: 1) the crisis was total (in the end, none would be spared its lash); 2) its solution would fill the lifetime of my generation and the next ones; 3) the one certainty about the solution was that the stages by which it was reached must be frightful, whatever the solution itself turned out to be.

A New Dimension

Does it sound wildly irrational to say that, when the newscaster broke into the ball game, I also laughed because that woman walked again across my mind's eye? It is so. With her began the prophecy; the circling of the scientific moon was implicit in her slow walk-past (though neither she nor I could know that). Yet to have lived with this prospect of reality for more than thirty years, and to have been unable to communicate it convincingly to others—that is the heart of loneliness for any mind. Cassandra knew.

It works out, too, in the simplest, most immediate ways. As soon as my wife and I were alone, I said: "They still do not see the point. The satellite is not the first point. The first point is the rocket that must have launched it." Of course, the scientists and the military chiefs grasped this obvious implication at once. But it took three or four days for anybody to say so, in my hearing.

In short, the struggle for space has been joined: But this was only the immediate, military meaning. Widen it with this datum: the satellite passed over Washington, sixty miles away. One minute later, it passed over New York. We have entered a new dimension. Like Goethe after the battle of Valmy, we can note in our journals: "From this day and from this place, begins a new epoch in the history of the world; and you can say that you were there."

There is a wonderful passage in the *Journal of the Goncourt Brothers*, wonderful, in part, for its date, which cannot be later than 1896. I shall not be able to quote it exactly from memory, but it goes much like this: "We have just been at the Academy, where a scientist explained the atom to us. As we came away, we had the impression that the good God was about to say to mankind, as the usher says at four o'clock at the Louvre: 'Closing time, gentlemen.'" None of us supposes that this moon means closing time. None of us can fail to see, either, that closing time is a distinct possibility. Again, the point is not that we do not yet have the ICBM fully developed; we will. The point is that the new weapons are, of their nature, foreclosing weapons, and, whether or not they are all presently in our hands, too, they are in the hands of others over whom we have no control. That is what I meant by "end of the world." Only those who do not know, or who do not permit their minds to know, the annihilative power of the new weapons, will find anything excessive in the statement. "Nine H-Bombs dropped with a proper pattern of dispersal" was a figure given me, three or so years ago, as the number required to dispose of "everything East of the Mississippi River." Whether the figure is accurate to a bomb or a square mile is indifferent. Any approximation of it speaks for itself.

Will to Inconsequence

Unlike Goethe, I doubt that any of us can feel a particular elation in being able to say: "And you were there." I suspect that about the best we can muster will be like the historic first words said to have been uttered by the King of Greece, on landing there after the German occupation in World War II and the ruinous civil war. "Nice weather for this time of year, isn't it?"

In those words, the end of dynastic Europe is, once for all, self-proclaimed. Their staggering inconsequence is not stupidity, but something much more final: the inability of a mind any longer to feel or know the reality which, by position, it should be shaping. Such a mind is no longer equal to the meaning of what is happening to it or to anybody else. Is not this condition growing on all of us? Is there not a deliberate will to inconsequence—a will not to know, not to see, the dimensions of what we are caught up in—a will to make ourselves, and our vision, small, in the child's hope that, if we work hard enough at it, we can make the tremendum enclosing us as small as we are? Perhaps, if we do not look, it will go away, leaving us with the Edsel and the split-level house. How else explain the fact that, born into a century unprecedented in scale, depth and violence of disruption (the two world wars and the new energy sources are instance enough), we nevertheless manage so successfully not to know its total meaning, but to see its shock piecemeal, as a disjointed, meaninglessly recurrent hodgepodge? The attitude is fixed in a habit of minimizing complacency, commonly couched as a posture of strength. But since it does not conform to the scale of real events, it is irrational, and leads, invariably, to those equally irrational spasms of extravagant jitter or extravagant optimism (such a wave as swept the West after the Geneva Summit Conference), whose inevitable recession in the face of the facts, plunges us into deepest puzzlement.

It is a late and tired habit of mind, which we seek to glorify by twining about it the rather dry and lifeless vine-leaves called: reasonableness, the calm view, common sense, the injunction never, under any circumstances, to feel strongly about anything (which, among other things, is blighting the energy of our youth at the source). "I believe," the little old man of twenty-one who was his college's most brilliant political science major, explained to me, "that the tendency, nowadays, is to see everything quantitatively." "Yes," agreed the Fulbright fellow who was with him, neither approving nor disapproving, merely baffled, but, above all, by my extraordinary question: "Doesn't the student mind ever get excited about anything anymore?" It is a positive will not to admit or permit greatness in event or men. But, since will itself implies a suspect energy, it takes form as a vague distaste, discomfort, distrust, relieved by a preference for the commonplace, the conforming, the small, the minutely (hence safely) measurable, the quantitative—method and dissection replacing life and imagination.

Imagination

Whatever else Sputnik is or means, the handwriting that it traces on our sky writes against that attitude the word: Challenge. It means that, for the first time, men are looking back *from outside*, upon those "vast edges drear and naked shingles of the world" which Arnold reached in imagination. In imagination—which is the creative beginning of everything (God Himself had first to imagine the world), the one indispensable faculty that has brought man bursting into space from that primitive point of time he shamblingly set out from. That breakthrough (all political considerations apart) touches us with a little of the chill of interstellar space, and perhaps a foreboding chill of destiny—a word too big with unchartable meanings to be anything but distasteful to our frame of mind. For it is inconceivable that what happens henceforth in, and in consequence of, space, will not also be decisive for what happens on the earth beneath. In short, Sputnik has put what was useful and effective in method and dissection once more at the service of imagination. It is the war of imagination that, first of all, we lost. It is in terms of imagination that the Russians chiefly won something. The issue has only been joined. Nothing is final yet. But it is joined in space, and it is at that cold height that henceforth we will go forward, or go nowhere. There is no turning back.

Before this illimitable prospect, humility of mind might seem the beginning of reality of mind. As starter, we might first disabuse ourselves of that comforting, but, in the end, self-defeating, notion that Russian science, or even the Communist mind in general, hangs from treetops by its tail.

November 16, 1957

The Left Understands the Left

The world is randomly streaked with comings and goings—the evidence of an intense activity, taking place largely out of sight. Sometimes, we catch glimpses of its passage. They are curiously suggestive. Usually they ask more than they tell. The comers and goers are, in general, public persons, but not, as a rule, official; though they may have been official a few moments ago, and may be official again a few minutes later. Such a public figure goes privately from America to India or Yugoslavia, for example—and sees whom; and what was said? A Soviet national comes to the United States in some unnoticed delegation, or one that is scarcely noticed, and, in any case, almost instantly forgotten. And, again, sees whom; and what was said? We are unlikely ever to know.

These half-glimpsed flittings fascinate by all they suggest, but do not tell. We can do little more than note them, though we may guess that, in the course of them, some little thread has been connected with some other thread, which, if we could see the whole web of the history of our time, might bear surprisingly on much that puzzles the mind about the underlying design.

Not long ago, I came on a little news item, dropped in more or less as filler—the brief news that Mr. Aneurin Bevan, on a recent trip to the Crimea, had been the house-guest of Mrs. Nikita Khrushchev. Presumably it was treated more fully elsewhere, but this was all that came my way. I found it a little nugget—one of those unnoticed bits of living history (unnoticed, certainly, by thousands living around me), which, like a bead of radium, lights up shoals of darkness, though the nature of radium remains a riddle, and what we see by its glow chiefly perplexes.

Mrs. Khrushchev perplexes. She is the wife of a man whose name, a year or so ago, was all but unknown to the West, but who in some six months has emerged as one of the most powerful men alive. The West knows so little about his wife that the discovery that she exists at all was something of a scoop. It is said that—another victim of "the cult of personality"—she passed some years in a Siberian slave labor camp. Khrushchev, meanwhile, stayed at home, as Stalin's Paramount Chief in the Ukraine or in the powerful Moscow Party section. He seems to have been able, or willing, to rescue his wife only after the Georgian's death. Some link this large restraint with the gossip that makes Elena Furtseva Mrs. Khrushchev's great rival. It seems to be true that Khrushchev moved his wife back from Siberia not long before he moved Furtseva into the Praesidium of the Soviet Communist Party.

Such Suetonian tales, perhaps a little true and largely silly, usually predispose us toward the wife. So does Mrs. Khrushchev's apolitical appearance. She looks like the type of peasant woman whom a Russian once described to me as: "A meal sack with a rope tied round the middle." (Of course, *that* Russian was not a Communist, but a Socialist Revolutionist; as solemn heads everywhere know, humor is the seed of heresy.)

Mrs. Khrushchev is burlier than the type, which tends to softness. In that plain, earthy face is read a vigor of the twofold kind that will rush in tears to rescue a kitten drowning in a rain-barrel, while snatching up, on her way, a chicken whose head she will, without pausing in her rush, tweak off, with the evening meal in mind. Of course, there is nothing exclusively Russian in that; peasants everywhere act much alike. Yet the Russian peasant does seem to have a special dialectic talent for combining opposites. A Yiddish writer summed it up to me this way: "A Russian peasant is a man who will go to endless pains to murder his grandmother by burning her alive in her hut. But then he remembers that the canary is also inside, and, at peril of his life, plunges into the flames to save the bird." A good deal that happens inside Russia is scarcely comprehensible in any other terms.

Yet I prefer something else. A former Russian anarchist, then old and gravely ailing, once showed me a little photograph of himself, taken in Tsarist days when he was in Siberian exile. In it, the sick man, stooping beside me over the picture, was seen as a youth, seated by a window filled with potted plants, in a Siberian *isba*. He was wearing a collared Russian blouse, and the lightly melancholy smile proper to his age, and to the revolutionist of that other age. The old man beside me mused: "The Siberians are not a mellow people, like the Russians; But, you see—there are flowers in the window. So, you see"—and here his voice dropped into that dying fall in which the Russian voice catches at times the weight of all this weary, unintelligible world—"so, you see, there is something gentle in those people, too."

What Did They Talk About?

Perhaps there is something gentle in Mrs. Khrushchev, too, if you are lucky enough not to be a chicken at meal time. What suffering she must have known and seen—revolution, civil war, famine, purges, murder of classes, nations, friends, world war, terror, terror, terror, such as hunting and hunted animals live in hourly—and, at last, a slave. This Lady Macbeth from Mtsensk might also say: "I have supped full with horrors." Is that what she said to Aneurin Bevan?

For, of course, it was his entrance under her battlements that made the news item seem to me a nugget. What was he doing in that galley? What was said across the *pertsovkas?* Aneurin Bevan, it is generally supposed, will be Britain's foreign minister—perhaps its next one—if the Labor Party comes to power, as it may do in two years time or less. (In Britain, prices are up 50 per cent in seven years; interest rates as high as 7, some say 8 per cent; gold and dollar reserves down $517 million in two months; good growing weather for Socialism.) Did they talk about that? Language would have been no barrier; they share a basic language. Keynes is a dialect of Marx not too greatly different than Slovene, say, is from Russian.

Did they talk about what, as foreign minister, Bevan might do to shoehorn Communist China into the UN; to pluck some feathers from the mutually detested conservative, the German Chancellor Adenauer; to coax American air bases out of Britain; to curb American thermonuclear prowess? It all falls under the plausible head of "relieving world tensions."

Or did they discuss common housekeeping details—the theoretical developments now being argued, heatedly within Western Socialism, violently within Communism? The nub of that debate is the question of how some individual freedom can still be had, and how much, while still having socialism. The degree to which Communism and socialism can approach each other over that bridge underlies one of the strategies implied in the theses of the 20th Congress of the Soviet Communist Party.

Did they discuss the tactical shift within British socialism whereby the Labor Party, with an eye to votes and much else, has shelved outright nationalization, at least for a while, in favor of a Socialist government's buying into key industry as majority stockholder; thus letting the old managers continue to do the work they do, in general, so much better than Socialist bureaucrats—namely, that of managing their own business, but as hirelings of the Socialist State? We can only guess. We are unlikely ever to know.

But we know this: Aneurin Bevan has long been a spokesman of that section of British socialism which has shrilly demanded that Britain's Conservative Government cease its development of thermonuclear weapons. "I see no purpose," Bevan recently (and shrilly) confided to Prime Minister Nehru about the H-Bomb, "in Britain arming herself with that useless weapon."

Turnabout at Home

We live and learn, especially if we have been to Mrs.

Khrushchev's. After his Russian visit, Mr. Bevan reversed his field to such effect that a motion putting the Labor Party on record against thermonuclear development was voted down 5 to 1 at the Party's latest Congress, with Mr. Bevan himself steering the steamroller amidst shouts of: "Turncoat," "Traitor," from that plangent minority which never learns that to gain power is what political parties first of all exist for. Why this turnabout? Well, you can scarcely elect an average Briton to vote for you as Socialist if, by doing so, he must also vote against his own thermonuclear self-defense. We are also told that, in Russia, Khrushchev gave Britain's presumptive foreign minister some specific Socialist advice: "Don't give up your Bomb and leave a vacuum." A vacuum? That is to say: Don't leave the United States, the one great power uncommitted to socialism, as the one thermonuclear power in the West.

Beyond that, what does this mean? I can only tell you what I think it means. Around 1951, one of the British Socialist leaders—Mr. Hugh Dalton, if I remember rightly—was urging on a Labor Party gathering a more conciliatory line toward the Soviet Union. In clinching his plea, he said: "The Left understands the Left." Yes, that is the crux of the matter. It is to say that, in the showdown, despite all brotherly invective and despite all brotherly arm-twisting, socialism still has more in common with Communism than either of these two has with conservatism. "Do not give up your Bomb and leave a vacuum." How that might work out with Mr. Bevan as foreign minister, in some tearing crisis of the East-West conflict, none of us knows. Neither is it at all difficult to imagine how it might work in terms of a Britain disposed by a justifiable self-interest to neutrality, and disposed by a Socialist government to conciliate Communism. The Left understands the Left.

November 23, 1957

"To Temporize Is Death"

"T his time last year," I thought. For the voice, asking its rather staggering questions over the long-distance wire, yesterday, was the same voice that had telephoned this time last year, almost to a day. It belongs to a friend who has spent a good many years in public life and public service. There was the same tenseness in his voice now as there had been a year before, but for reasons as different as if, in the meantime, the world had spun over on its axis and reversed its poles. Then the voice had seemed to me curiously optimistic (the Hungarian revolt was on). Now it seemed to be speaking from the bottom of a pit (Sputnik II had been launched the day before). Until that moment, I had not realized, could scarcely have believed possible, the degree of alarm that the second Communist moon had stirred in the West.

The voice said: "Suppose the Russians have one hundred rockets of the thrust that launched the second Sputnik, and that the rockets have hydrogen warheads. Suppose they are trained on the United States. Will the Russians first give us an ultimatum in the hope of taking our technology intact? Or will they launch the rockets without any ultimatum? Certain quarters," the voice went on, "have put that question to their Communist experts. What would your answer be?" As put to me, it was a purely personal, unofficial question; I am not a Communist expert. Perhaps that is why, instead of reaching for a graph, I thought: "This time last year . . ." Let us remember that time a little, because it bears both on my friend's question and my answer.

This time last year, I came out of my workroom, one morning, to find my wife waiting, shaken and distracted, just outside. "They've come back," she said. "They're bombing the city. It's

24

horrible." It was Sunday, November 4, 1956. The Soviet armor had wheeled back on Budapest. We listened to the pleas for help from the Hungarian resistance radios; boosted, rebroadcast or paraphrased by the stations of the West. One appeal broke off: "May God help you and help us." "At that point, the Hungarian station went off the air," said the American announcer's Sunday voice—comes out like a ribbon, lies flat on the brush. At that point, in fact, the man with the tommy-gun had kicked in the door, and it required no imagination at all to know what had happened next in that Hungarian studio. My wife burst out: "Why don't they stop those horrible commercials! Why don't all the stations pray, why doesn't everyone simply pray to God to help the Hungarians? Poor people, oh, poor, poor people!" She rocked back and forth silently in order not to give way further to her grief.

I said nothing. I was thinking of what the West would do, or, as I surmised, would not do, with this historic opportunity. I was remembering certain words of Lenin's at the great turning-point of this century. He was warning his sluggard henchmen that history sometimes gives men one chance, and that it seldom gives them a second chance; that, for resolute and intelligent men, given that chance, not to seize and act upon it is "crime"; that "to temporize is like death," "to temporize *is* death."

This time last year, the temporizing UN was trying to try to push through a resolution condemning the Hungarian horror; was screaming moral indignation, though somewhat like the duck in *Peter and the Wolf,* "from the middle of the pond." This time last year, the voice that telephoned me yesterday called from Washington to ask hopefully: "What do you think? Will we intervene in Hungary?" I said: "No intervention. The people are afraid it means world war. If you could put it to a vote, you would not get one thousand votes for intervention in the whole country." The figure might just as well have been one million votes without in any way changing the fact.

This time last year, I wrote, to try to fix, first of all, the physical image of those events while they were happening, and then certain of their wider meanings, but also, perhaps, out of the need that sometimes makes men scrawl last-minute notes that may never be read and set them adrift in bottles that may never be found. So I wrote: "There are names that belong to the language of destiny, and one of them is Budapest—Budapest of the November days. In hallways, civilians huddled over machine-guns—men as watery with fear, you may be sure, as all others who have gone against Communism, not with words only, but with acts. On the streets, half-grown boys, darting bare-handed against Soviet armor, to stuff flaming rags in the tank vents. Patrolling the shattered housefronts, children with slung rifle and tormented faces. On the public squares, the ranged bodies of the fallen, already nondescript in death, and stared at by the nondescript living of a kind that always clots around the raw edges of action. A late autumn landscape of an age that certainly supposes itself to be some kind of summit of accomplishment."

"A Phase of Hope"

This time last year, I wrote: "Here, on the Hungarian and on the Polish plain, history is struggling to break in two. A phase has been arrested, which (visibly) from Teheran and Yalta through the Communist conquest of China, and (incalculably) in every direction beyond, has been one of piecemeal disaster to mankind. In its stead, there has opened the possibility of a phase of hope, still highly unstable and inconclusive. In this new region of experience, the Hungarians hold the first heights of meaning. The mind cannot enter here from the West except by way of Hungary, any more than you can enter Thermopylae from the south without passing that marker which, after two thousand years, still says to those who may have forgotten every other fact about the Persian Wars: Stranger, tell the Lacedemonians that we lie here, obeying their command.

"This is not because the center of political gravity in the satellite situation lies in Hungary. Events are likely to disclose that it lies, as it has from the first, in Poland and in the Germanies (West as well as East). Least of all is it, as we have so often heard of late, because Soviet action in Hungary has at last stripped the mask from Communism and revealed its true face. Anybody who had to wait for Budapest to tell him that does not know what century he has been born into. Nothing has happened in Hungary by way of horror that has not happened repeatedly within the Communist Empire, and more humbly. Millions of Russians (let us remember) have already been destroyed, defying Communism. Their struggle and their cries were lost in the distances of Euro-Asia. But we *heard* the Hungarians, and they tore at least at our nerves.

"Those cries command our attention first to a challenge that is as simple as it is timeless. All other factors change or fade—the politics, economics or their catchwords that men defied or defended. But resistance enacts a human meaning that is always the same. It says that when man, the sufferer, rises by courage above the odds of pain, he liberates by his act the one force that brute power, destroying all else, is powerless to destroy. There is more. To the exact degree in which brute power is most incontinently brutal, those who resist compel it to collaborate in dramatizing that meaning. That done, resistance, though it can be crushed, cannot be defeated. Disaster is not defeat. Resistance outlives disaster because the sons remember the fathers, and that memory is caught at again and again by others who suffer, and whom it moves to dream of resisting in their turn. This is the dialectic of hope; it stirs in darkness."

This time last year, I wrote: "But there is not just one challenge. There are two of them. It is not only Soviet power that the Hungarians have challenged. They also confront the West with a challenge equal to, or greater than, their challenge to Communism. The history of the past forty years has been marked by this incongruity: that Communism, permanently strife-torn and precarious, and weak in most material ways beyond anything imaginable to the average experience of the West, has repeatedly stood off or scored off a West in most material ways immensely more powerful. Until Communism detonated its A and H Bombs, it was never a question of comparative power. Power, on the part of the West, was never lacking. Will was lacking. And that failure of will was matched by a failure of intelligence, taking form as an inert complacency, varied recurrently by sweeps of illusion that Communism was about to change into the exact opposite of what it is, into the opposite of all that has given it power and empire, into something more like that image that the West cherishes of the West, something more eligible for the garden party guest-list. This of the most consistently implacable revolution in history. It is to that failure of will and intelligence in the West that the Hungarians have cried: 'Halt!', challenging it to reverse its forty-year retreat by giving it precisely what most it dreads—an opportunity."

But at last I pushed those pages to one side. Who, in the West, would read in them anything but overblown feeling; as if revolution for Communism or against it, were ever made by anything less than feeling, running molten under the pressures of necessity. But feeling does not, as one of our fondest notions has it, keep the measuring mind from measuring narrowly the reality of what it feels about. I knew before I had finished writing that, within weeks, what I was writing about would be as dated as if it dealt with another age.

The opportunity had been given and it had gone. Autumn had frozen into winter. The Hungarian revolution had passed into the stricken twitchings of the general strike. The West continued to babble about it—some jumble of initials or words that meant that a second revolt might occur in the spring. What does the West know of the pathology of revolution, let alone the pathology of a revolution defeated, which converts at once into mean commonplaces of a kind that make no colorful news stories—the help-lessness, grief, and induced terror of those who have had the mis-chance to survive fathers, brothers, sons, who have been shot, jailed, or have simply "disappeared"? Or the unheroic monotony of no food, fuel, gas, electricity; the grimy misery of cold, con-tinual, sapping cold; and the colder knowledge, gained by so hideous a trial and error, that no help is coming from anywhere, not in time, not in any way that counts. The defeated almost never revolt twice—not in quick succession. Nor did we need any expert to tell us this. One Hungarian resistance fighter had packed it all into one sentence; not bitterly, either, but with the simple statement of fact which is more impaling. He said: "You did not organize even a gun-running service for us."

And This Year

So, yesterday, one year later, I answered to this effect the startling question of the voice that had asked so different a question, this time last year: "If the Russians have one hundred ICBMs trained on us and mean to use them—then, in my fallible opinion, you can be quite sure that there will be no ultimatum. The Russians will launch the rockets first and talk afterwards, if there is any-body left worth talking to. On the other hand, again in my fallible opinion, the Russians do not have one hundred such rockets trained on us. Nor do I believe that such saturation attack forms any part of over-all Communist strategy at this time. Communist strategy seems to me to have quite different procedures and ends in view, geared to a close, forty-year scrutiny and experience of the West."

"For once," said the voice, brightening, "you are more hope-ful than I am." I said: "That is not hope." I meant this: Budapest convinced me that the will and intelligence of the West are still unequal to what besets them, and this regardless of the sumptu-ousness of our retaliatory power. What price retaliatory power if, having it, you must stand by, lacking the will or ingenuity to improvise "even a gun-running service for us"? I take it to be a matter of simple fact that the retaliatory power of the Strategic Air Command still offsets any temporary thrust ahead of Communist rocket prowess—as the President has assured us in the first of his "chins-up" talks. Retaliatory power is a simple necessity of survival. But retaliatory power keeps rocketing into ever more terrifying stages of stalemate. And there is probably a limit, not easy for the layman to grasp, beyond which these sprints into progressive stalemate can sprint no farther. Even now, neither side dares break the relative stalemate except in the certainty of consequences so frightful that imagination rejects as pointless the effort to picture them.

Forward motion in either direction would seem, therefore, to lie outside the central stalemate. This is a revolutionary conflict we are locked in, and, in it, we are, perforce, compelled to act as much as revolutionists as the enemy, though in a different way.

For victory must presumably go to him who succeeds in overleaping or bypassing the weapons stalemate, and swinging to his side decisive population masses and their economies now beyond his control. This is the strategic thrust of the theses of the 20th Congress of the Soviet Communist Party, now personified in the leadership of Nikita Khrushchev. That is what, at the moment, the Middle East is about. This is why what I can see by Sputnik II's dim light alarms me less than it alarmed my telephoning friend and millions of others. It is why, instead, I look back from Sputnik II to Hungary, this time last year.

Some years ago, I met in an unlikely executive office, high in a New York skyscraper, a little group of men, introduced namelessly as leaders in America of a Hungarian resistance movement. I did not know why we had met and I do not know now. The modern world is like that. But suddenly the spokesman for the rest asked me: "Do you know what is America's secret weapon?" I said: no. He brought his hand with unexpected force against his chest as he answered: "We, *we* are your secret weapon."

In the days of Budapest, I thought often of that odd conversation. I thought, too, that, if we were holding it again, I should have put a question in my turn. I should have asked: "Do you think we shall know how to use our secret weapon?" But I should have spared them from answering by answering myself: "Neither do I." The moment when the West, by action, has made that answer untrue, will, I suspect, mark a turn in history quite as decisive in its way as Sputnik II.

December 28, 1957

Big Sister Is Watching You

Several years ago, Miss Ayn Rand wrote *The Fountainhead*. Despite a generally poor press, it is said to have sold some four hundred thousand copies. Thus, it became a wonder of the book trade of a kind that publishers dream about after taxes. So *Atlas Shrugged* had a first printing of one hundred thousand copies. It appears to be slowly climbing the best-seller lists.

The news about this book seems to me to be that any ordinarily sensible head could possibly take it seriously, and that, apparently, a good many do. Somebody has called it: "Excruciatingly awful." I find it a remarkably silly book. It is certainly a bumptious one. Its story is preposterous. It reports the final stages of a final conflict (locale: chiefly the United States, some indefinite years hence) between the harried ranks of free enterprise and the "looters." These are proponents of proscriptive taxes, government ownership, Labor, etc. etc. The mischief here is that the author, dodging into fiction, nevertheless counts on your reading it as political reality. "This," she is saying in effect, "is how things really are. These are the real issues, the real sides. Only your blindness keeps you from seeing it, which, happily, I have come to rescue you from."

Since a great many of us dislike much that Miss Rand dislikes, quite as heartily as she does, many incline to take her at her word. It is the more persuasive, in some quarters, because the author deals wholly in the blackest blacks and the whitest whites. In this fiction everything, everybody, is either all good or all bad, without any of those intermediate shades which, in life, complicate reality and perplex the eye that seeks to probe it truly. This kind of simplifying pattern, of course, gives charm to most primitive story-telling. And, in fact, the somewhat ferro-concrete fairy tale the author pours here is, basically, the old one known as: The War between the Children of Light and the Children of Darkness. In modern dress, it is a class war. Both sides to it are caricatures.

The Children of Light are largely operatic caricatures. In so far as any of them suggests anything known to the business community, they resemble the occasional curmudgeon millionaire, tales about whose outrageously crude and shrewd eccentricities sometimes provide the lighter moments in Board rooms. Otherwise, the Children of Light are geniuses. One of them is named (the only smile you see will be your own): Francisco Domingo Carlos Andres Sebastian d'Anconia. This electrifying youth is the world's biggest copper tycoon. Another, no less electrifying, is named: Ragnar Danesjöld. He becomes a twentieth-century pirate. All Miss Rand's chief heroes are also breathtakingly beautiful. So is her heroine (she is rather fetchingly vice president in charge of management of a transcontinental railroad). So much radiant energy might seem to serve a eugenic purpose. For, in this story as in Mark Twain's, "all the knights marry the princess"—though without benefit of clergy. Yet from the impromptu and surprisingly gymnastic matings of the heroine and three of the heroes, no children—it suddenly strikes you— ever result. The possibility is never entertained. And, indeed, the strenuously sterile world of *Atlas Shrugged* is scarcely a place for children. You speculate that, in life, children probably irk the author and may make her uneasy. How could it be otherwise when she admiringly names a banker character (by what seems to me a humorless master-stroke): Midas Mulligan? You may fool some adults; you can't fool little boys and girls with such stuff— not for long. They may not know just what is out of line, but they stir uneasily.

The Children of Darkness are caricatures, too; and they are really oozy. But at least they are caricatures of something identifiable. Their archetypes are Left Liberals, New Dealers, Welfare

Statists, One Worlders, or, at any rate, such ogreish semblances of these as may stalk the nightmares of those who think little about people as people, but tend to think a great deal in labels and effigies. (And neither Right nor Left, be it noted in passing, has a monopoly of such dreamers, though the horrors in their nightmares wear radically different masks and labels.)

In *Atlas Shrugged*, all this debased inhuman riffraff is lumped as "looters." This is a fairly inspired epithet. It enables the author to skewer on one invective word everything and everybody that she fears and hates. This spares her the plaguey business of performing one service that her fiction might have performed, namely: that of examining in human depth how so feeble a lot came to exist at all, let alone be powerful enough to be worth hating and fearing. Instead, she bundles them into one undifferentiated damnation.

"Looters" loot because they believe in Robin Hood, and have got a lot of other people believing in him, too. Robin Hood is the author's image of absolute evil—robbing the strong (and hence good) to give to the weak (and hence no good). All "looters" are base, envious, twisted, malignant minds, motivated wholly by greed for power, combined with the lust of the weak to tear down the strong, out of a deep-seated hatred of life and secret longing for destruction and death. There happens to be a tiny (repeat: tiny) seed of truth in this. The full clinical diagnosis can be read in the pages of Friedrich Nietzsche. (Here I must break in with an aside. Miss Rand acknowledges a grudging debt to one, and only one, earlier philosopher: Aristotle. I submit that she is indebted, and much more heavily, to Nietzsche. Just as her operatic businessmen are, in fact, Nietzschean supermen, so her ulcerous leftists are Nietzsche's "last men," both deformed in a way to sicken the fastidious recluse of Sils Maria. And much else comes, consciously or not, from the same source.) Happily, in *Atlas Shrugged* (though not in life), all the Children of Darkness are utterly incompetent.

So the Children of Light win handily by declaring a general strike of brains, of which they have a monopoly, letting the world go, literally, to smash. In the end, they troop out of their Rocky Mountain hideaway to repossess the ruins. It is then, in the book's last line, that a character traces in the air, "over the desolate earth," the Sign of the Dollar, in lieu of the Sign of the Cross, and in token that a suitably prostrate mankind is at last ready, for its sins, to be redeemed from the related evils of religion and social reform (the "mysticism of mind" and the "mysticism of muscle").

That Dollar Sign is not merely provocative, though we sense a sophomoric intent to raise the pious hair on susceptible heads. More importantly, it is meant to seal the fact that mankind is ready to submit abjectly to an elite of technocrats, and their accessories, in a New Order, enlightened and instructed by Miss Rand's ideas that the good life is one which "has resolved personal worth into exchange value," "has left no other nexus between man and man than naked self-interest, than callous 'cash-payment.'" The author is explicit, in fact deafening, about these prerequisites. Lest you should be in any doubt after 1168 pages, she assures you with a final stamp of the foot in a postscript: "And I mean it." But the words quoted above are those of Karl Marx. He, too, admired "naked self-interest" (in its time and place), and for much the same reasons as Miss Rand: because, he believed, it cleared away the cobwebs of religion and led to prodigies of industrial and cognate accomplishment.

The overlap is not as incongruous as it looks. *Atlas Shrugged* can be called a novel only by devaluing the term. It is a massive tract for the times. Its story merely serves Miss Rand to get the customers inside the tent, and as a soapbox for delivering her Message. The Message is the thing. It is, in sum, a forthright philosophic materialism. Upperclassmen might incline to sniff and say that the author has, with vast effort, contrived a simple materialist system, one, intellectually, at about the stage of the oxcart, though without mastering the principle of the wheel. Like any consistent materialism, this one begins by rejecting God, religion, original sin, etc. etc. (This book's aggressive atheism and rather unbuttoned "higher morality," which chiefly outrage some readers, are, in fact, secondary ripples, and result inevitably from its underpinning premises.) Thus, Randian Man, like Marxian Man, is made the center of a godless world.

At that point, in any materialism, the main possibilities open up to Man. 1) His tragic fate becomes, without God, more tragic and much lonelier. In general, the tragedy deepens according to the degree of pessimism or stoicism with which he conducts his "hopeless encounter between human questioning and the silent universe." Or, 2) Man's fate ceases to be tragic at all. Tragedy is bypassed by the pursuit of happiness. Tragedy is henceforth pointless. Henceforth man's fate, without God, is up to him, and to him alone. His happiness, in strict materialist terms, lies with his own workaday hands and ingenious brain. His happiness becomes, in Miss Rand's words, "the moral purpose of his life." Here occurs a little rub whose effects are just as observable in a free enterprise system, which is in practice materialist (whatever else it claims or supposes itself to be), as they would be under an atheist Socialism, if one were ever to deliver that material abundance that all promise. The rub is that the pursuit of happiness, as an end in itself, tends automatically, and widely, to be replaced by the pursuit of pleasure, with a consequent general softening of the fibers of will, intelligence, spirit. No doubt, Miss Rand has brooded upon that little rub. Hence, in part, I presume, her insistence on "man as a heroic being" "with productive achievement as his noblest activity." For, if Man's "heroism" (some will prefer to say: "human dignity") no longer derives from God, or is not a function of that godless integrity which was a root of Nietzsche's anguish, then Man becomes merely the most consuming of animals, with glut as the condition of his happiness and its replenishment his foremost activity. So Randian Man, at least in his ruling caste, has to be held "heroic" in order not to be beastly. And this, of course, suits the author's economics and the politics that must arise from them.

For politics, of course, arise, though the author of *Atlas Shrugged* stares stonily past them, as if this book were not what, in fact, it is, essentially—a political book. And here begins mischief. Systems of philosophic materialism, so long as they merely circle outside this world's atmosphere, matter little to most of us. The trouble is that they keep coming down to earth. It is when a system of materialist ideas presumes to give positive answers to real problems of our real life that mischief starts. In an age like ours, in which a highly complex technological society is everywhere in a high state of instability, such answers, however philosophic, translate quickly into political realities. And in the degree to which problems of complexity and instability are most bewildering to masses of men, a temptation sets in to let some species of Big Brother solve and supervise them.

One Big Brother is, of course, a socializing elite (as we know, several cut-rate brands are on the shelves). Miss Rand, as the enemy of any socializing force, calls in a Big Brother of her own contriving to do battle with the other. In the name of free enterprise, therefore, she plumps for a technocratic elite (I find no more inclusive word than technocratic to bracket the industrial-financial-engineering caste she seems to have in mind). When she calls "productive achievement" man's "noblest activity," she means, almost exclusively, technological achievement, supervised by such a managerial political bureau. She might object that she means much, much more; and we can freely entertain her objections. But, in sum, that is just what she means. For that is what, in reality, it works out to. And in reality, too, by contrast with fiction, this can only head into a dictatorship, however benign, living and acting beyond good and evil, a law unto itself (as Miss Rand believes it should be), and feeling any restraint on itself as, in practice, criminal, and, in morals, vicious—as Miss Rand clearly feels it to be. Of course, Miss Rand nowhere calls for a dictatorship. I take her to be calling for an aristocracy of talents. We cannot labor here why, in the modern world, the pre-conditions for aristocracy, an organic growth, no longer exist, so that impulse toward aristocracy always emerges now in the form of dictatorship.

Nor has the author, apparently, brooded on the degree to which, in a wicked world, a materialism of the Right and a materialism of the Left first surprisingly resemble, then, in action, tend to blend each with each, because, while differing at the top in avowed purpose, and possibly in conflict there, at bottom they are much the same thing. The embarrassing similarities between Hitler's National Socialism and Stalin's brand of Communism are familiar. For the world, as seen in materialist view from the Right, scarcely differs from the same world seen in materialist view from the Left. The question becomes chiefly: who is to run that world in whose interests, or perhaps, at best, who can run it more efficiently?

Something of this implication is fixed in the book's dictatorial tone, which is much its most striking feature. Out of a lifetime of reading, I can recall no other book in which a tone of overriding arrogance was so implacably sustained. Its shrillness is without reprieve. Its dogmatism is without appeal. In addition, the mind which finds this tone natural to it shares other characteristics of its type. 1) It consistently mistakes raw force for strength, and the rawer the force, the more reverent the posture of the mind before it. 2) It supposes itself to be the bringer of a final revelation. Therefore, resistance to the Message cannot be tolerated because disagreement can never be merely honest, prudent, or just humanly fallible. Dissent from revelation so final (because, the author would say, so reasonable) can only be willfully wicked. There are ways of dealing with such wickedness, and, in fact, right reason itself enjoins them. From almost any page of *Atlas Shrugged*, a voice can be heard, from painful necessity, commanding: "To a gas chamber—go!" The same inflexibly self-righteous stance results, too (in the total absence of any saving humor), in odd extravagances of inflection and gesture—that Dollar Sign, for example. At first, we try to tell ourselves that these are just lapses, that this mind has, somehow, mislaid the discriminating knack that most of us pray will warn us in time of the difference between what is effective and firm, and what is wildly grotesque and excessive. Soon we suspect something worse. We suspect that this mind finds, precisely in extravagance, some exalting merit; feels a surging release of power and passion precisely in smashing up the house. A tornado might feel this way, or Carrie Nation.

We struggle to be just. For we cannot help feel at least a sympathetic pain before the sheer labor, discipline, and patient craftsmanship that went to making this mountain of words. But the words keep shouting us down. In the end that tone dominates. But it should be its own antidote, warning us that anything it shouts is best taken with the usual reservations with which we might sip a patent medicine. Some may like the flavor. In any case, the brew is probably without lasting ill effects. But it is not a cure for anything. Nor would we, ordinarily, place much confidence in the diagnosis of a doctor who supposes that the Hippocratic Oath is a kind of curse.

May 31, 1958

Springhead to Springhead

The independent farmer, says one of their number, is doomed to lose his fight against bureaucracy; but it was worth making and will not be forgotten

Westminster, Md.—After winter's long, cold enemy occupation, spring is back; no longer halting and promissory, but true, irreversible spring. Now the springheads, dried up in last summer's fierce drought and long silent, burst out again, refilled by this spring's plentiful moisture, and rush on their way to the sea with a chance of drowning babble in babble as they pour past Washington (we are in the Potomac watershed). Now the voices of the fertilizer and lime purveyor and the farm implement hucksters are heard louder than the voice of the turtle in the land. "Make five blades of corn grow where one grew before," they coo. "Let 140 bushels an acre (with fertilizers) swell farm surpluses which 40 bushels (without fertilizer) could never swell so prosperously. Let one man do (with machines) the work that three could scarcely do (without). So disemployment thrives." Of course, they do not really say these things; this is only the logic of what they say.

And, as throughout nature in the spring voice answers voice, their voices are answered by others. These are the voices of the Agriculture Department's employees, and other official and semi-official farmers' helpmeets. There are enough of these turtles in the land so that, if there were time at this season to count noses, I suspect that the bureaucratic nose count in almost any farm county would fill you with wonder at how they manage without colliding. In part, they manage by a division of labor. While some (bringing, often, a good deal of expert knowledge and patient solicitude to jobs, in general, poorly paid) are helping you multiply yields—others (the land-bankers and that ilk) are exhorting you to decrease yields. They will pay you for it, too; and so painlessly that some scarcely notice that the hand which reaches for the payment is thereafter meshed in the controls. Since few seem to mind this, or to notice the gaping paradox—the coos of increase cancelling the coos of decrease—perhaps it hardly matters. Yet history, glancing back, may be struck by another paradox and wonder if, in America, it was not in the countryside that socialism first took firm root and stooled.

The Bureaucrat Tactic

It has been a carefully nurtured growth. The earlier controls (Roosevelt and Wallace *consulibus*) were rather flirtatious things. Bureaucracy was chiefly feeling out the land to see how many inches it could take before reaching for a mile. On this farm, we were always careful to plant less than the official wheat allotment. But the great tactic (it is almost a reflex) of the bureaucrat mind is to keep things unsettled, to keep you off balance, to make you feel unsure. So I was not surprised when, one day years ago, a small character knocked at the door to say that he was the wheat inspector, that he had been looking over our fields (of course, without asking), and that we were overplanted. His thin, sidewise smile tried to hint at least hanging at sunrise. It disturbed my wife. But I knew that we were not overplanted, and, I thought I knew what silver cord connects bureaucracy and politics. "Elections are coming up," I said to her. "You can be absolutely sure that nothing more will be heard of this." Nothing was, of course.

But, shortly afterwards, I happened in on a neighbor who is made of sterner stuff. It was hog-feeding time, and he approached with a pail of slop in each hand. I asked: "Did that fellow look over your fields?" My neighbor set down each pail, somewhat with the air of a President laying a State of the Union message on a lectern; and eyed me for a moment of dense silence. Then he said: "You know he's a black-hearted skunk," adding with immense relish: "I run 'im." I thought I heard the fifes of '76.

You will not hear them now, or, I think, again. Those days, around Pearl Harbor, were a simpler, sweeter time. Besides, the Second World War, with mass armies and half a world to feed, made nonsense of controls. It remained for this Administration to weld them on. I have never known on just what remote, snow-capped Olympus the wheat allotments were alloted. Official notice of how much (or how little) wheat you could henceforth lawfully plant just arrived, one day, in the mail. But, if you had been alloted less than fifteen acres (most of us were), you could not afterwards vote about continuing or discontinuing this control. Voting about that was henceforth the privilege of the bigger planters. Those under fifteen acres were henceforth stripped of a vote in this rather relevant matter. Moreover, if you planted above your official allotment, even if the yield of the overplant was not for sale, was used wholly to feed your own stock or poultry, you still had to pay a penalty for growing it. Moreover, government surveyors could come into your fields at any time, to measure your wheat acreage and determine what penalty you must pay. This, you will see, went considerably beyond controls in the earlier sense, which most farmers had been content to abide by if only, by doing so, they would be let alone; while some, in the vain hope that the surest way to be let alone was not to take even the subsidies to which controls entitled them, refused these.

So it happened, now, that a few such farmers, who held that their land was inviolable, and that the day of the *kolkhoz* had not yet arrived made known their temperatures by running up, at the entrance to their farms, signs which read: "Government agents keep out!" There was a tiny farm revolt hereabouts, with some strong feelings and words between embattled farmers and officials. And these farmers were certainly mistaken; at least about what hour of history it is. The years of bureaucratic feeling-out were over. The day of submission-or-else had come. The Administration moved swiftly against the resisters in a legal action known (ironically enough, it seemed to some) as: *The People v. Morelock.*

You can read about this particular Morelock in *Witness*, where I wrote of him and his family: "Names to be written rather high, I think, on the column which is headed: 'And thy neighbor as thyself.'" In sum, the charge was interfering with government agents in pursuit of their duty. Mr. Morelock and his fellow defendants won that action, on a technicality, rather, I suspect, to the relief of the bureaucracy, which wanted no martyrs; and whose chief purpose, after all, was not to harass or penalize farmers. What was wanted was to seal on controls and cut surpluses, and this the resistance threatened over-all.

One Man's Resistance

It was a silly, hot-headed, inconsequential resistance? It did not reflect the feelings of masses of farmers anywhere? There is a point of view—nowadays we tend to exalt it as "reasonable"—from which any spontaneous resistance on principle, and against odds, is seen always to be silly. And such struggles often appear inconsequential enough at the time. Those who make them are few in number if only because those who react fiercely on principle are, in the nature of men, likely to be few. Nor are they, in the nature of themselves, likely to be worldlywise, to have thought out in crisp detail all the implications of their action. If they could do this, presumably they could not act. For their drive to act is organic and instinctive, not neatly cerebral. So their opponent finds it easy to dismiss them as crackpots and extremists; and, in general, his strength is defined by the degree to which he can afford to dismiss them with the derisive smile. The smile mantles power.

Perhaps I should make a point clear: I was not directly concerned by any of this. Some time before, when we saw that controls were coming to stay, we simply stopped planting wheat. But

I could not bear to see my friends mauled. So I spoke privately to the wife of one embattled farmer. I went to the wife because I did not wish to sustain the man's hurt or blazing anger at what I had to say. In effect I said: "Urge him to stop. He cannot win. He will only destroy himself, and for nothing. This cause was lost before it began." These people are strong human types of a kind little known among the mystic circles of the intellectuals. They hate a quitter, and they do not make a quick distinction between a faint heart and the coldly measuring glance. I saw dawning in this woman's eyes, first shock that I, of all people, should say this; then a tinge of just-repressed contempt. "That is not what you did in the Hiss Case," she said. I said: "No. That is why I am saying this to you. Do not destroy your lives for nothing."

Then I went away. I did not return until the action was over; all had simmered down, and reality had taught what words seldom can. For these people have a strong grasp of reality, a simple wisdom of the earth, where ten minutes of unseasonable hail will tear to ribbons a year's corn—but you go on from there. By then, they knew (whether or not they would admit the fact in words) that they were the defeated. They were proud to have made the effort; and I think that this pride was about in ratio to their realization that they could only have been defeated; no other issue was possible. It was their pride to have acted, anyway. Into that pride they retreated. This was no retreat from principle. The retreat was into silent conformity to superior force, the force of the way things are, which compels compliance, but convinces no one. In ending their resistance, they yielded to that force, but from their silence they looked out at it with unyielding scorn.

I asked the woman to whom I had first spoken: "What now?" She answered that, when the Republican Party was first organized, her forebears (they had always lived on this same farm) had voted for Fremont. When, just before and during the War Between The States, Maryland was rent, they had twice voted for Lincoln. They were Black Republicans; in the whole history of the line, they had never voted anything but Republican. She said: "We will never vote for a Republican again." I said: "What do you gain by that? Do you suppose those others [the Democrats] will not give you more and tighter controls?" She said: "Then we will never vote again at all." Never is a long word. But, in so far as anything can be certain in an uncertain world, I think it is certain that these people—they are of the breed of those who built the nation from the unpeopled earth—will never vote again. They have silently seceded, not so much from the electorate (that is only the form the gesture takes), but from what they believe to be betrayal of basic principle, without which their world surrenders a part of its meaning. That principle is the inviolability of a man's land from invasion even by the State, the right of a man to grow for his own use (unpenalized by the State) a harvest which his labor and skill wrings from the earth, and which could not otherwise exist. Freedom was at stake, of which the inviolable land and its harvest were symbol and safeguard. The word "indivisible" is not one that these people commonly think or speak with. So they do not think or say: "Freedom is indivisible." But that is what they sensed and that is why they acted. It was not controls, but coercion, they resisted.

Crisis of Abundance

Do not misunderstand me. I do not suppose that wheat allotments, or similar controls, are inherently wicked, or that government's action in enforcing them was wrong—given our reality. I believe them to be inescapable, which is something different. The problem of farm surpluses is, of course, a symptom of a crisis of abundance. It is the gift of science and technology—improved machines, fertilizers, sprays, antibiotic drugs, and a general rising efficiency of know-how. The big farm, constantly swallowing its smaller neighbors, is a logical resultant of those factors (big machines are fully efficient only on big acreages). Surpluses follow. So does the price trend of farm real estate, steadily creeping upward for decades. So does the downtrend of the farm population (it has fallen by a million in about two decades).

If farmers really meant to resist these trends, to be conservative, to conserve "a way of life" (as they often say), they would smash their tractors with sledges, and go back to the horse-drawn plow. Of course, they have no intention of doing anything so prankish, and, moreover, would not be let do it if they tried. Controls would, appear at that point, too. For the cities, which dominate this society, are dependent on machine-efficient yields. So the State would have to act to prevent the farmer from preserving "a way of life," just as it has to act by controlling, in the field, an agriculture of anarchic abundance. Both are actions against anarchy. Controls of one kind or another are here to stay so long as science and technology are with us; or, until the ability of farmers to produce and the ability of the rest of us to consume their product is again in some rough balance, thus ending the problem. That balance will be restored, presumably, in the course of a survival of the fittest, in which efficiency determines survival. And efficiency is itself the result of a number of factors, one of which is almost certainly size of operation. In short, the farm unit tends to grow bigger and more efficient, as the farmers, growing more efficient, too, grow drastically fewer in necessary numbers.

This is the only *solution* of the farm problem; one that is obviously impersonal and rather inhuman (and in that it is exactly like any other comparable development in history, for example the development of the factory system). Short of that solution, no man or party can solve the farm problem. They can only contrive palliatives. All that men and parties can do is to try to mitigate and soften, in human terms, the plight of the farmer in the course of heading toward that impersonal solution which science and technology impose. Hence controls and the incipient socialism of the countryside which controls imply and impose. This is the basic situation, however much incidental factors may disguise, blur, or even arrest it for longer or shorter terms. That is why the mass of farmers go along with controls which, almost without exception, they loathe. Who will say, that they are not right?

Yet neither do I believe my neighbors were wrong to resist. I believe they were right, too—and on a plane which lies beyond controls. In my heart, I believe that no resistance on principle, where freedom is the principle involved, is ever meaningless, or ever quite hopeless, even though history has fated it to fail. For it speaks, not to the present reality, but to the generations and the future. And, in so far as it speaks for freedom, it speaks for hope. Freedom and hope—they are the heart of our strength, and what we truly have to offer mankind in the larger conflict with Communism that we are also locked in.

It was not the initial resistance that I was urging my neighbors against in this case, but an unwise persistence in it. I thought that resistance, once enacted, was well done and full of meaning for us all. I thought that, thereafter, swift disengagement was simple common sense, since neither the battle nor the war could be won—not in this season of history. The fewness of the resisters, their summary defeat, the way in which their struggle passed largely unnoticed and was quickly forgotten, seemed to bear out this view.

A Great Continuity

It also chilled me. It seemed to me that, with the defeat of these farmers, a retaining wall had fallen out. And this not only in the sense that hereby the enveloping State had made a new envelopment, and that, to that extent, the whole outwork of individual freedom and its safeguards was weakened. The real portent was the complacent consensus that it scarcely mattered. No one was stirred. No one really cared. No one rose to say that when, at any point, the steadily advancing State retrenches the rights and freedom of any group, however small, however justified the retrenchment is in terms of impersonal reality, every man's security is breached. That, tells us what hour of day it is.

That is why, I think, it is not wholly cranky or idle to remember, with each returning spring, this episode. Not that I think it will be forgotten. The land has a long, long memory. Nothing is much more thought-provoking than to listen—in barns where men meet and talk on days too wet to work, in farm kitchens on winter nights—and hear the names of men and women long dead (names which, in life, were scarcely known beyond a radius of 30 miles) come to life in conversation. They live again in most precise detail—tricks of manner, speech, dress, foibles, follies, generosities, integrities, courage, defeats. Often such recollections are laced, in the telling, with much human malice. Yet even this, at its worst, has the effect of brushing the grass on many an otherwise neglected grave. And, by that touch, is restored a great continuity—the same from the beginning of the earth, through the mentioned dead, to those who mention them. A nation is also its dead. As if any of us lived otherwise than on the graves of those who gave us life, who, so long as we conserve them in memory, constitute that generative continuity. Among such memories, surely, will remain, like a germ in a seed, the little farmers' resistance. Perhaps in some more fully socialized spring to come, someone, listening to that recollection, will pause over it long enough to ask himself: "What was the principle of freedom that these farmers stood for? Why was the world in which this happened heedless or wholly unconcerned? Why did they fail?"

Perhaps he will not be able, in that regimented time, to find or frame an answer. Perhaps he will not need to. For perhaps the memory of those men and women will surprise him simply as with an unfamiliar, but arresting sound—the sound of springheads, long dried up and silent in a fierce drought, suddenly burst out and rushing freely to the sea. It may remind him of a continuity that outlives all lives, fears, perplexities, contrivings, hopes, defeats; so that he is moved, to reach down and touch again for strength, as if he were its first discoverer, the changeless thing—the undeluding, undenying earth.

September 27, 1958

Some Untimely Jottings

With millions of other TV-viewers, I watched the President give his UN address on Arab slum clearance; a well-organized speech, and rather gallantly delivered, besides—only, almost wholly irrelevant. The rate at which things are moving is glimpsed in the fact that nothing whatever had been settled about the crisis in the Middle East, before we put it largely out of mind in favor of the current crisis in the Far East, which had overtaken it. Later, Mr. Eisenhower gave us his views on that one.

Groping for the sense behind the President's words, I came up with nothing better than: didn't say he would, didn't say he wouldn't. Since the speech was beamed to Moscow and Peking, quite as much as to you and me, this, I presume, was exactly the effect intended: keep them guessing. Alas, they are rather good at guessing. Besides, they know the secret in the daisy, the secret in each crisis. Seldom has a secret been less of a riddle. The rhetorical issues in each crisis are almost never the point. Neither the freedom of the Lebanon nor the title deeds to Quemoy is the point. In each crisis, there is only one point to be settled, and it is always the same point: whether or not the West has resolved at last to stop the Communist advance in the only way it can be stopped: by a decision to make war at need.

Of course such war, at this stage of stalemated history, could only be in the nature of an adventure. Doubtless there are those, on both sides, who are impatient to end the intolerable stalemate by risking the adventure. But, since the consequences to both sides are foreseeably apocalyptic, it seems unlikely that the adventurers will have their way. For nobody needs to guess about the thermonuclear consequences.

It is this that leaves the veteran guessers in Moscow and Peking free to guess (like the President) that there will be no world war over Quemoy. Hence the wrenching pathos which is what I, for one, chiefly carried away from both the President's addresses, namely: a sense that he and his advisers, doing the very best they know how, could still, in effect, do so little. Never imagine that their plausible critics could do more. Those critics might do it all somewhat differently. That is to say—unless they, too, had taken firmly the frightful decision for war at need—they might conduct the alternative retreat more gracefully, trippingly, wittily in the style of the Adlai-an adlib. It is unlikely that they could accomplish anything more effective in a situation whose extremity is defined by its two alternatives: fight or retreat. That is the only secret in the daisy.

If this is true, but there is to be no war—what then? Mercifully, I am not required to guess.

But I should like to stick my neck out interspatially by guessing about something else, lest, one of these months, we suffer another Sputnik-type alarm at the expectable. I should like to guess that the Russians are fairly content to leave to us the vast cost and effort of shooting the moon. Instead, I should guess that the Russians are investing every available resource of mind, material, money, in getting men into space and back again, alive. Like the rest of us, they have heard that whoever first learns to commute to and from space, and to man something or other up there, will presumably control space, and much else besides.

War on the scale of the worlds, annihilation, space and its command, a visible nearness to the brink of unheard-of disaster. We know that it is scarcely farther away than an initiating impulse in the whorls of a brain responsible for ordering a responsible hand to push a button, and so set in motion the marvelous mechanisms for inflicting or resisting chaos. We are continually told about it. We listen, and in part believe. In larger part, the reality passes us by; it passes our imagination. Too big. Too big truly to grasp. One day, a meaning of it comes home in a form we can grasp—the distress of a single human creature and his reflections on it. A friend writes: "Up at 5 a.m. today to get some hot coffee into my son and drive him to his draft board in time (for the Army vehicle which was picking up the quota). If the time should ever come (as I pray it never will), when you have to take this journey with your son, I think you will consider with a quite new urgency what Jaspers meant in writing: 'Quietly, something enormous has happened in the reality of Western man: a destruction of all authority, a radical disillusionment in an over-confident reason, and a dissolution of bonds that makes anything, absolutely anything, seem possible . . . Philosophizing, to be authentic, must grow out of our new reality, and there take its stand.'"

"Quietly, something enormous has happened in the reality of Western man." I am constantly baffled because so few seem to grasp this enormity of our situation, which is defined by the certainty that there is no way out of it that can possibly be simple, easy, familiar, usual, in terms of anything we have known before. Whether the resolution of our total crisis is to be unimaginably violent, or what, at this moment, seems even less imaginable, a massive peaceful settlement, what comes next can only be tremendous. We are visibly at a point of change, a turning point, which has not its like in history. Henceforth, peace implies consequences almost as staggering as war.

October 11, 1958

R.I.P., Virginia Freedom

I do not know how many people gratefully knew, or knew of, Virginia Freedom—Mrs. Leon Freedom—who died in Baltimore recently. Thousands, I should think, though she never made sensational headlines.

I remember vividly our first encounter. It was shortly before the first Hiss trial. In a Baltimore department store, my wife and I became aware that someone was staring at us—a handsome woman, somewhat in the Valkyrie style. Then the Valkyrie asked shyly: "Mr. C?" I conceded, and she said: "I must talk to you." Oblivious of jostling shoppers, the stranger talked. Her tale was of skulduggery on high, purporting to show how matters were being rigged against me. There was indeed mischief afoot, and she had come on traces of it.

That was Virginia Freedom's way. Her sources of information were sometimes surprising. She had been a newspaperwoman (traces of the ordeal lingered in certain easy oddities of speech). To an uncommon intelligence, she united an almost inexhaustible memory, a volcanic zeal in research and a wide-ranging political interest (geopolitics was almost her undoing). She put them all into the service of fighting Communism. During the high days of the anti-Communist hearings, Mrs. Freedom (and a few friends) constituted themselves a kind of gadfly squad, erupting into legislative offices, and even into the Senate dining room, to exhort weary law workers, to supply background, leads and guidance. She was mistress of a good-natured sarcasm, and her accounts (with gestures) of Senator Needless To Name and Congressman You Know Who, being bemused by the simpler complexities of revolution, were often sidesplitting. (It was also possible to feel a certain compassion for the encircled legislators.)

I used sometimes to think of Mrs. Freedom as Thurber's heroine, with the shotgun across her knees, saying: "There isn't going to be any revolution!" Certainly not, if Virginia Freedom could stop it. She was a rallying force, and her energy had a rush and momentum that swept others along and kept them going in the worst of times. Yet, in careful sum-up, she could no more deceive herself about political realities than about political people. So she had, in reflective moments, a very sober view of the odds in the East-West conflict and the predicament of the American Right. But there was nothing cheerless about her. Fun burst into any room she entered, and continued, playing, sometimes hilariously, sometimes searchingly, over whatever she was girding at. A bigness, range and jollity of mind that seemed simply a superflux of that teeming energy—that is how Virginia Freedom will be remembered.

Mrs. Freedom died of a heart attack—in her sleep, the sovereign boon.

November 8, 1958

A Reminder

A watchful reader notes that I closed a recent piece in this magazine by saying: "We have visibly reached a point of change, a turning-point, which has not its like in history." He also recalls that I used the same phrase several years ago, in an article (about the 20th Congress of the Soviet Communist Party) in *Life* magazine. "You rang several changes on it then," he writes. "Does this phrase have some mystic meaning for you, not known to the rest of us? Is it an incantation? Or is it just that you can't think of anything else to say?"

I suppose that, in a way, it is an incantation, in the sense that it is meant to evoke something—to be a reminder of something though it is never identified—so that readers, coming on it, may feel a little uneasily: That theme again. I have used it deliberately somewhat like that leitmotif which, now and again, stirs under the dense overcast of Wagnerian sounds to remind us that Fate is still at work.

Though we late-comers are scarcely any longer aware of it, one of Christianity's tidings of great joy was that it had banished Fate from the world. No longer was a man's Fate fixed and shaped irreversibly by the stars he happened to be born under, so that his life was predestined to be just so, and not otherwise. The moving finger writ, and all his piety and wit could not cancel out one fated circumstance; so that the noblest posture, for slave (Epictetus) and Emperor (Marcus Aurelius) alike, was a stoic resignation. This was the glad tidings—that Fate was overthrown. The hopeless entrapping ring was broken. Man himself could break it, since every individual soul was divinely precious. Armed with this knowledge, man was free at last, first of all from Fate; then free to make of his destiny what he would and could.

In our century, Fate has returned to the world, and possessed the minds of millions who, submitting to its thrall or acting in its name, seek to extend its dominion. This time, Fate has returned in the guise of History. It may be put (very loosely) like this: History is shaped by the action and interaction of great impersonal forces. Men merely enact it. If they act, prevailingly, in the direction of the main lines of force, its momentum carries them along to success; and we are invited to call such men great, wise, and even good. Those who, out of folly, ignorance or stubborn principle, resist the main lines of force, History exterminates mercilessly. They are in the way; and what does a ragweed, for example, have to do with mercy, when a million pollen grains may be wasted to bring a single seed to fruition? The process is impersonal.

There is grandeur in this concept. It is idle to fancy that we can dismiss it with a snap of the fingers or by snapping shut our minds against it. Nor can we easily frown it down by a stately assurance which, very often, is not truly assured. For we see the main design and workings of the concept enacted on all sides of us, in Nature. Why should Man be the exception? Prove it. Nor is this concept at home only in the Communist East. It exists widely throughout the West, nameless, or under various distracting names, as a floating ambience, breeding a climate.

The Choice

Thus, at a basic point of issue, the mind of the West is divided against itself; and this basic division is repeatedly rubbed raw as it is touched by each of our recurrent crises, at all levels. For this is the basic cleavage. It is this which, behind the teeming crises, the overtoppling threat of great disaster, not only in the form of bombs and missiles, gives to our mood a hovering sense of finality that no amount of rationalizing quite dispels. It is this which sometimes makes us feel as if there were occurring in the general mind of man something like a molecular rearrangement of particles; that man is about to become something other than he is, if he does not perish in the process. Behind all events and all appearances, *this* choice is presented: Fate or Freedom. And it is presented as an issue that must be decided—now. It is this which gives us that sense of living through a time which has not its like in history.

The phrase is not mine. It was spoken in our own lifetime, by a particular, fateful man in the spin of this century's moment of decision. I am assuming that the Russian Revolution was the decisive action of the century's first half, in the sense that, directly or indirectly, it affected everything of importance that came after. I should like to identify the man and the moment as I felt their impact close to the time when both converged. What follows is from an unpublished manuscript:

I was thirteen years old when Sir Edward Grey, then Britain's Foreign Secretary, stared into the dusk of the day in 1914 when England declared war on Germany, and summed up for his age: "The lights are going out all over Europe tonight. They will not be lit again in our time."

I was sixteen when, on an October day in Petrograd—the rain-wind beating in from the Finland Gulf—Antonov-Avseenko, at the head of the Red Guard, rushed the Winter Palace. Therewith, all power in the former empire of the Czars fell to Communism. In the Petrograd Soviet Leon Trotsky rose to report the revolutionary victory. As if (for once) at a loss for language, he stared for a moment through his glasses at the mass of capped, greatcoated, high-booted men who stared back at him. Then he found the words equal to the event: "Comrades of the Soviet of Workers' and Soldiers' Deputies, we have this day begun an experiment that has not its like in history."

This is where the phrase comes from. This is the formal announcement that Fate had returned to the world in the guise of History. This is why I use the fateful phrase, from time to time, to remind others, without expressly laboring it, of a choice that it will surely be granted to each of us to make in this time, first in our mind, then in our acts: Fate or Freedom.

November 22, 1958

A Republican Looks at His Vote

The housewife ahead of us was in the polling booth so long, I thought she could not just be splitting her ballot; she must be emulsifying it. It turned out that she was trapped (voting machines are still something of a novelty with us). When she pushed the lever to the right, the curtains had closed behind her. She could not remember how you open them again. She could not call out (decorum forbade); and she could not get out (panic was taking over). I missed the big moment of her liberation by a bipartisan rescue team. I was watching the voting queue.

Something was noticeable in the faces of the voters—a peculiarly braced sobriety. They seemed to me the faces of people who had, some time before, firmly and finally made up their minds, and were here to do something about it. I had not the slightest doubt as to what most of them meant to do.

Nevertheless, I would vote with my Party. I always vote like a Democrat—that is to say, I always vote a straight Party ticket, but Republican. In that way, I understand myself to be furthering, at least until it becomes simple historical idiocy to do so, certain general propositions about the world—propositions which, on this most recent election day, seemed remarkably remote and unreal.

So voting did not take me a minute. I read only one name (J. Glenn Beall) to locate the Republican line. I snapped down all the Republican keys and left the booth, feeling as if I had thrown my vote into the gutter. No doubt, a man who seeks to act in and on reality, rather than to stand still and watch from some fastidious sideline, must, of necessity and more than once in his life, consciously throw something very precious in a gutter.

I took my little self-disgust, which was only the private face of a larger concern, out into the golden autumn weather that was so ironically like the weather of election day, 1952. Our naive fervors of 1952 appear wildly comical in the disenchanted light of 1958. The discrepancy helps to measure, I think, where six years of "middle of the road" (or twilight sleep) Republicanism have brought some of us.

The morning before that other election day, I was ill. There was a family hubbub. We all knew what was wrong. But we were also deeply concerned about something else. We supposed that the vote between General Eisenhower and Adlai Stevenson might be close, and we felt that Stevenson's election would be a disaster. Therefore, every vote counted. Perhaps you must have gone through the school of the Revolution to take voting so seriously as we do; to feel that, in a sense, there is no longer such a thing as a merely American election because every election and its outcome here is an event in the world conflict. Every vote contributes to a cumulative outcome that bears directly on the fate of hundreds of millions of people elsewhere, as well as our own.

So that day in 1952, somebody said: "But you can't have a heart attack *now*. You've got to vote tomorrow if we have to take you there on a stretcher." As I walked away from the polling place in that same autumn sunlight, I was struck down.

By evening, an ambulance had got me to a hospital, which, by one of those wonderful fumbles that occur, turned out to be the wrong hospital. While everybody tore inside to straighten matters out, my stretcher lay on the ramp; and I could hear voices close by, talking election. A blanket had been pulled (prematurely) over my face. Later, I clawed my way through drugs and made out foggily a small bare room and a little nurse, sitting in one corner. When I stirred, she jumped up and asked if there was anything she could do for me. I said: "Tell me how the election turned out." She hesitated, disappeared, reappeared almost at once, and said: "A landslide for Eisenhower." I stopped fighting the sedative and fell most peacefully asleep.

On this last election night, we sat—my wife, my son and I—listening to the remarkable TV coverage. My son, who had just cast his first vote, was clearly exhilarated by the scale of the event he was witness to. He knew, at least in a general way, that he was seeing the incipient third phase of that American social revolution of which the New and Fair Deals had been rocket stages one and two. My wife, as the returns piled up, huddled deeper in her chair. "Gloom" could not possibly cover what she felt. It was rather that she knew she was watching the Republicans epitomize one of the Bible's most cruelly piercing insights: "To him who hath shall be given. But from him who hath not, even that little which he hath shall be taken away." I was almost wholly unmoved. I had "discounted" the news. "It is not Fortune that governs the world," Montesquieu has told us. "There are general causes, moral and physical, which operate in every monarchy, raise it, maintain it, or overturn it."

If this is true of monarchies, it is also true of parties. The Republicans had lost touch with reality in all directions, and in all groupings, until domestic policy resembled irresolution tempered by expediency, and foreign policy more and more resembled something like eccentricity. They had been handed a disaster.

January 31, 1959

Some Westminster Notes

S omebody said, the other day, when we were talking about the new jet service to Europe, that in twenty or thirty years people will be traveling abroad by rocket. New York will then be fifteen minutes from Paris, or closer than the Empire State Building seems ever likely to be to Rockefeller Center by Fifth Avenue bus. Nobody saw anything wildly improbable in the notion.

Still, the mind is not yet committed to the shortest distance between two points as invariably the best of all possible ways to get somewhere. The mulish mind may still prefer detours, precisely because they digress.

Just before Christmas, somebody sent me a French book, part of whose leisurely title reads: *Five Essays on the History of Ideas in Russia and Europe*. Essay I begins: "Between 1758 and 1762, Koenigsberg was occupied by Russian troops under General Fermor. In the old Collegium Albertinum—as the university was called—a thirty-five-year-old professor, of somewhat timid appearance, announced a course in physics for 'Messieurs, the Russian officers.' "

This was news to me and I found it fascinating. As if the author invited us to peer into the least likely of peepholes, and what we saw, incredulously, was the dark backward and abysm of time, with (somewhere down below) the greatest of all human centuries (I mean, of course, our own), squirming, germlike, at one of its countless, forgotten points of origin—Koenigsberg, 1758.

This is not just because Koenigsberg, easternmost of provincial German towns, has lately been next-door neighbor to Peenemunde, the experimental rocket base. Nor is it because, even more lately, we have seen Koenigsberg become Kaliningrad, not merely Russian-occupied this time, but annexed outright as the westernmost of Soviet cities. Nor is it that the timid-looking science teacher was Immanuel Kant, "unknown as yet even in Germany"—the author (to be) of *The Critique of Pure Reason*, schoolmastering the forerunners of the enveloping East. What arrests is rather (with the Sputniks in mind) the thought of Russian officers, enlivening the tedium of that earlier occupation by getting up their physics. And, indeed, physics and politics have been in curious (and often violently unstable) mixture throughout the last 200 years. Not only in Koenigsberg—or, see your morning newspaper.

And with that, the mind is off on a little ramble. With the Koenigsberg classroom as center, it scans the horizon of that time in search of anything else that may be curiously lurking in it. The mind stops, arbitrarily, with a child.

In 1758, Lazare Carnot was only five years old. Who gives a thought to Carnot today, though he was an engineering and military head of the first rank, of whose achievements Napoleon made full use, but whose genius Napoleon's masks, somewhat as Bach's so long masked Buxtehude's? It would be some years after Koenigsberg before Carnot whipped up his first important paper: *Essay on Machines in General*. A few years more, and he would organize from scratch, and in one year, the French Revolution's fourteen armies; and, almost singlehanded, elaborate their innovating strategy and tactics. Accomplishment enough so that, when the many tongues that wag in the many heads that do not think, cried out for his arrest during some terrorist spasm, they could be silenced by a single voice which asked: "Would you dare to lay hands on the organizer of victory?" So Fate, who now and again prefers irony to the knife, let Carnot live, to die an exile in Schoolmaster Kant's Germany.

To Lavoisier, who is on the Koenigsberg horizon, too—his first interest physics, like Kant's Russian officers'—Fate turned the cutting edge. That brilliant brain was cancelled at the neck by the guillotine—the murderous technical improvement that the Revolution contributed to progress, along with certain other innovations that are with us still. For example, conscription, mass armies, the concept of the nation in arms (in part Carnot's brainchild, and necessity's).

True, in our day some have sought to undo that business of mass armies. Among them, a master of French prose and author of a treatise, celebrated chiefly among specialists: *Vers une Armée de Métier—Toward a Professional Army*. The master of prose (and of much else French at the moment) is, of course, General Charles de Gaulle.

With that the circling mind has circled back to the thoroughfare of here and now. And just in time for some sensational traffic. For while I was shuffling these bits and pieces, the Russians sent up that rocket which, missing the moon, has gone on, they tell us, to orbit the sun. 1758 to 1958 plus two. Lunik, Kant (of all people), facing an all but forgotten roomful of Russian officers. At last the impulse takes form in a trajectory that bursts Earth's gravitational field. A wall has fallen. Nobody knows how many other walls, of the mind, of reality, fell with it, unnoticed. Which reminds me that, in the far-off 1920s, one of my fellow undergraduates had this to say of (and to) his age:

Once in unpeopled Nineveh,
Where no one heard the sound,
The human-headed bull of god,
Crashed outward to the ground.

Such ways, the solitary mind
Strains backward, year on year.
Are all the walls at Nineveh
Whose crash we do not hear?

February 28, 1959

Missiles, Brains and Mind

Without a national revolution in our attitude toward creative mind, the mass production of intercontinental missiles and technical brains will not prove enough to assure our survival

"What Does Not Destroy Me . . . "

Thousands, perhaps millions, of us have been following, as closely as possible, the great weapons debate whose epicenter is in the Congress. That debate breathes a rancid tone of political partisanship. This is extremely disquieting. On the other hand, without that political animus it is possible that there would be no debate. That would be more disquieting still. I, for one, hold the belief that at least a majority of literate men and women are pretty shrewd at separating what is politically motivated (or distorted) from the reality of the situation which emerges from the argument. And it is this reality that none of us can afford to miss or widely misunderstand.

This debate goes (as Germans say) *um Tod und Leben*—for life or death. Not only is the basic reality of the situation it evokes awesome; it is peculiarly perilous because the reality is so novel that many cannot credit it. They simply cannot take it seriously. That reality is, of course, that, for the first time in our history, the nation as a whole is coming under the possibility of direct, annihilative attack. Our continental fortress is no longer unreachable; our ocean moats have shrunk or may serve to float toward us the submarine conveyors of disaster. The rockets have done this.

Therefore, what we are truly debating is our survival as a people that wills to remain sovereign and not subject—as the people that we are and will to be, and not what someone else wills to make us. Let us, for the moment, table all brave talk about our special breed of freedom and this or that high moral issue, as all luxuries go overboard in combat, which, in the resolving clinch, never turns on these, but on the necessity for raw survival. This is what we are debating: survival.

The debate is especially difficult for most of us to follow efficiently because: 1) much of it concerns regions of science and technology which, as laymen, we are simply not competent to grasp; and 2) much of it turns on scraps and echoes of conflicting information which, for good reasons, we are not permitted to know in full, and, again, might well not be competent to evaluate if we did know it. But most of us feel competent to see that the conflict forks out from two main Intelligence questions.

Oldest Rule of War

One of them is what our Intelligence tells us about the state of Soviet weapons progress. The other concerns our own rate of progress, past, present and tomorrow. Neither is clear. In addition, opinions about these matters cannot be simple. Naturally, they involve many more (and much more complex) factors than whether the Russians are ahead of us in certain respects and behind in others; whether, at this moment, they can match us rocket for rocket, or outmatch us, etc., etc., etc. But the oldest, simplest rule of war would seem to dispose of much of this part of the debate. The rule is: never underrate your mortal enemy. Do not, if you can help it, overrate him; but far better to overrate than underrate.

Just here, there emerges from the debate another point which almost any literate layman can claim competence to see and call decisive. The point is this: whatever the precise state of Russian rocketry and missile production, or our own, the Russians have achieved approximate destructive parity with us. This would seem to mean that, whether or not either nation has the power to inflict near total extinction on the other, each has the power to ruin the other. And that would seem, to those who may lie under such ruins or inherit them, to be about all that is necessary.

As someone has remarked, the real horror of an atomic war is not the fate of millions who may be fried in a flash; the real horror will be the fate of those who survive to haunt the ruins. If, as seems to be the case, people exist who still fail to grasp what this apocalypse implies, perhaps it is well to remind them of a colloquy (on TV, several months ago) between Mr. Dave Garroway and one of the top-ranking generals responsible for giving the signal to retaliate in event of atomic attack on us. The Q. and A. went much like this:

> MR. GARROWAY: "General, in your opinion could we survive such an attack?"
> THE GENERAL: "Yes, I think so."
> MR. GARROWAY: "How long would it take us, after such an attack, to get back to where we are now?"
> THE GENERAL: "Perhaps a couple of hundred years."

They were not trying to frighten little children. They were trying to make big children face reality.

Approximate destructive parity would seem to be all that is necessary for another reason. I happen to be one of those who believe that, barring hideous folly or human failure, these ruins will never come to pass. I cannot possibly document this belief; and neither can anybody else who holds (extremely tentatively, of course) this view. But it is not just fantasy. It derives from conclusions (drawn from Communist theory and decades of Soviet strategy and tactics in action) that Russian missiles are primarily political, not primarily military, weapons. The last thing, in my tentative opinion, that the Russians want to do with their missiles *at this time* is to launch them against the United States. For parity, by definition, works both ways. The Russians are not romantics, and have no greater whim than we have to become a continental ruin—especially since the ruins after an atomic war will not even be worth looking at.

The purpose of the Soviet missiles is, first, to erect a deterrent fence around the Communist heartland. For some reason, some of us seem unable to realize that the Russians are also afraid of us. But, finally, and much more important, the purpose of the Soviet missiles is to impose on the West a truce of exhaustion, taking form in one or another degree of atomic disarmament. No need to recap here the perils for the West of such a truce. My colleague, James Burnham, has long and patiently pointed them out in explicit detail. On the other hand, the depth and ferocity of the world crisis is measured by the fact that the atomic stalemate forced the East-West conflict into space in order to continue it on the scale of that new, fluid dimension.

Two Points Overlooked

The question is inescapable: How long can this go on, how far, and to what end? I find no comfort, because I put little credence, in the complacency of those who say: We can outlast and outplay the Russians at this game. This seems to me to overlook (among others) two instantly visible points. It assumes 1) that the Russians are competing only in the rocket field and not in others, where, in general, they have been more successful than we have been to date. It overlooks 2) that a formidable enemy, seeing itself dangerously outclassed, might be driven to desperation. In that case, the rockets might, at that moment, cease to be primarily political, and become in fact primarily military weapons. With that we are back at those ruins.

The larger probability would seem to be that neither power can long sustain a decisive over-all weapons headway of the other; but that, by spurts, now one, now the other, will draw ahead in some feature of this mortal race. Of course, this leaves out the possibility of the development of a defense, at least partially effective, against rockets. I am told, pretty reliably I believe, that we are in fact hopefully engaged in such a project. If this is true, you can be reasonably sure that so is the vigilant enemy. But such defense, too, works both ways, and would seem again to bring us to a point of partial standoff without, however, ending the weapons and space race.

Obviously, this cannot be ended while either side is racing. For if it is true that Soviet missiles are primarily political, we cannot therefore cease trying to catch up and overtake Soviet progress. To do so would also be hideous folly; would again, instantly, and more certainly than any desperation, convert the Soviet rockets from political to prime offensive weapons of immediate aggression. We can only do our utmost to outmatch the presumed Soviet lead. In this matter, I find myself thinking more like a Democrat than like many of my more tranquilized fellow-Republicans; and this, both as to belief in the necessity of supposing that a Soviet lead exists and may widen, and the necessity of sparing no effort or cost to close the weapons gap.

But, at that unsparing point, certain consequences also appear, which my mind refuses not to face as part of our total reality. As the weapons and space race climbs ever more steeply in cost and effort over years, it is scarcely conceivable that the pull should not begin to be felt by every American in constrictive ways, which, if pushed (and there are plenty of pushers around, gleefully waiting for a pretext) must radically transform our way of life. The Russian missile and space program is paid for directly out of the pockets, hide and hopes of the Soviet citizen. True, Russia began from hunger while we still have wads of affluent fat to melt off before the pinch is cruel; and the strong-arm State must enforce those ultimate sacrifices which State power exists to enforce. Is it conceivable that it will not come to this, even among us? It will be simple necessity; and necessity is its own imperative sanction.

Mikoyan's Message

I submit that this is one reason why certain businessmen, who sense clearly enough the grim shape of things to come, appeared to listen with closer attention than did certain hopefully socializing labor leaders, to what Anastas Mikoyan flew so far to tell us, namely: that Russia wants to end the Cold War. I submit, too, that this was what Mikoyan chiefly came to say, and that all else— verbal ticklings of the German question; or talk of trade contingent on credits; or the relaxing of our restrictions on certain exports; or a passionate interest in supermarketing and the packaging of potato chips—was incidental to that one simple statement: Russia wants to end the Cold War. The commissar had only to repeat it as frequently and publicly as possible since, above all, he was saying it over the heads of the Administration to the people as a whole. Nor was this just a random tactic of divisive mischief. This kind of deception applies a tactic rooted in Communist theory and successfully tested in four decades of Soviet practice.

But the prospect of political and economic changes among us is not the only transformation we might bear in mind as an ultimate consequence of the space and weapons race. There is another transformation, which is much more certain, and certain to come much faster. Usually, this one is discussed in terms of American education and its inadequacies. In some circles, it has become almost a sport to cite the discrepant figures which tend to show how many more scientists, engineers, etc., etc. the Russians are yearly graduating than are we. It is a deadly sport. For, if the figures are generally accurate (and, again, for our own skins' sake it is well to assume that they are), they spell out a portent. It is, of course, that in a comparatively short time the Russians will have produced a massively outnumbering elite of the kind on which the security and progress of modern States depend. Nor is this, again, a sudden, spastic lunge on the Russians' part. Again, the development of such an elite derives directly from Communist theory and the Communist world-view. Those who would like to glimpse what the enemy is up to, could do worse than dip (for a starter) into Friedrich Engels' polemical work commonly called the *Anti-Duehring*.

In general, the problem appears to be viewed as simply one of education, in an almost automatic sense. "Give us the funds, the necessary physical plant and the proper teachers' pay," goes the refrain in which can be heard the deep hunting bay of the Education lobby in full cry—"Give us these, and we will mass-produce the brains." And, certainly, these needs must be met if brains are to be mass-processed.

Yet it seems possible, too, that the problem does not turn wholly on the academic processing of what we loosely call "brains." It would seem to turn, at least as critically, on the much more difficult problem of what we loosely call "mind." I suggest that the implied presence in the latter word of reflective and creative imagination, rare and elusive as a trace metal, measures some difference of meaning between the two terms. Practical brains we have always had, and of an organizing genius whose scale and audacity have made America one of the wonders of history. Mind, in the sense I have suggested, is something else again, not, perhaps, because it is necessarily in short supply, but because something like a national revolution in our attitude to it must occur before it can become effective.

Revenge of the Mind

Almost a decade ago, Henry Regnery, the publisher, and I sat with some others in (appropriately, perhaps) the Douglas MacArthur suite of a Midwest hotel. There were no Sputniks in the sky that year. Yet there was a shared feeling that something was radically wrong in the land, which the conversation tried, fumblingly, to get at. Somebody said: "America has always secretly despised the mind. Now mind is taking its revenge. We need it desperately; and it simply isn't there." A sweeping criticism, but not nearly so critical or so sweeping as the evidence which has since crested in our missiles lag. The energy of practical brains, backed by the immense resources of our technology, may make good that lag, which, in default of sovereign and imaginative mind, was not foreseen—together with much else. It is a basic attitude toward mind, quite as much as education, that needs transforming. Such basic transformations are, admittedly, harder to make, and take longer, than mass-processing a dozen campus generations, or even closing a missiles gap. But there seems no valid reason to suppose that necessity will not breed what survival requires. That is one root challenge of our ordeal.

While we are mastering it, we might do worse than curb those recurrent twinges of fear that secretly (and sometimes openly) beset us, by fixing in our heads the insight that the great diagnostician of this age added to the grammar of courage: "What does not destroy me, makes me stronger."

May 9, 1959

The Hissiad: A Correction

The author of Witness *denies saying Alger Hiss 'has paid his penalty.' Far from it: 'The wound is there, and its poisons continue to drain through the system.'*

The ever-helpful press has been at it again, this time in the matter of Alger Hiss' decision to go to Europe, and the State Department's decision to issue him a passport for the purpose. Press treatment of this news reached a fine blossom in the paragraph with which *Newsweek* (April 20) wound up its story about the Hissiad: "At the weekend, endorsement of Hiss' travel plans came from an unexpected source. 'Alger Hiss is an American citizen who has paid his penalty for the crime of perjury,' said Whittaker Chambers. 'He has every right to apply for and receive a passport.'"

Whatever the intention, the effect of this paragraph is mischievous. Still, left to myself, I should probably have let it pass without comment. Why single out one item more than another from the quota of distortion that daily passes for news? But good friends insist that this one will deeply puzzle, and even dismay, many people. I am afraid that anybody of whom this may be true is in for a good deal of nervous shock, though for better cause, before this century ends. But I also agree that there are matters about which people have a right not to be puzzled and dismayed unnecessarily. So, for what good it may do, here goes.

Newsweek's paragraph begins with a fumble ("endorsement"), and ends, I am afraid, with a misquotation. Perhaps it can be said of *government* that it "endorsed" "Hiss' travel plans" to the extent that issuance of a passport supposes a considered decision. It cannot possibly be said of me. I have no competence whatever to "endorse" the Hiss plans, no means, no desire; nor, for that matter, any particular interest in a project about which I know nothing beyond the wispy report. I may (and do) speculate that this journey was a predictable next step in that public reorbiting of Mr. Hiss which is so precious a cause to his partisans, among them certain fairly formidable national figures. Beyond that speculation, the report that Alger Hiss is going abroad excites me no more than the news that several thousand other tourists are, even now, poised for the annual pilgrimage ("Ah, Venice—the Leaning Tower!").

Of course, I was aware from the first buzz what fanciful chigger would be inflaming the press just below the skin. For have we, even yet, learned anything that matters about these things, and how they work, and why? I seriously doubt it. Anyway, telephoning newsmen promptly produced the expected chigger in the form of the expected question: "Is *he* going behind 'the Iron Curtain'?" I said: "Of course, *he* isn't going behind 'the Iron Curtain'." Question: "Why do you say that?" Answer: "I must ask you not to press me on the point. You can easily figure it out for yourself." In short, if, for a decade, and in spite of everything, you had been insisting that you never were a Communist, you would scarcely, at first chance, streak for the Communist Empire. Mr. Hiss could find little that would serve his turn in going to Moscow; and neither would Moscow.

My guess would be that Hiss will home on London, to lay a wreath (figurative, at least) on the grave of the late Lord Chief Justice, who, for somewhat cryptic cause, was moved to write a handsomely slanted book in his favor. In Britain, Hiss has long had many partisans, literate, righteous, opinionated, and, in this case, completely muddled, as only clever English minds can sometimes be. There will be an epergne on the luncheon table.

Now to that part of *Newsweek*'s paragraph in which I claim to be misquoted. It consists of the words: "[Alger Hiss] has paid his penalty for the crime of perjury." I do not believe that I said this because I do not believe it (except in the shallowest legalistic sense) to be true. So I am as certain as anyone can be, in the absence of transcript, that I could not have said it, even in the haste and annoyance of answering foolish questions. That is not the way the matter presents itself to my mind.

Hiss and the Truth

History and a lengthening lifetime have left me too uncertain on the general subject of society, and the question of debts to it, or penalties, for me to have put the case like that. Society and the least man in it are too bafflingly manifold, the chances of birth and heredity, of time, place, environment and history, too incalculable, for such easy packaging. Moreover, the Scriptural injunction not to judge is not only compassionate; it is almost self-servingly prudent. We never pass judgment on anything or anybody without, by that act, in the same instant, defining our own human limitation. The act of judging always, mercilessly, judges, first of all, ourselves.

Of course, it is true—life does not permit us to live, for the most part, in such terms. We live on the world's terms, and act within their web of reverend compromises. But, in those terms, I can think of few men of whom it seems to me less possible to say that he has paid any effective penalty than Alger Hiss. In his case, a penalty was exacted, and a suffering was incurred. But the horror of it derives only in the last instance (though it sounds heartless to say so) from Hiss' suffering as an individual man. The true horror of it lies in the fact that, on his side, the penalty and the suffering were sheer waste. There is only one main debt, and one possible payment of it, as I see it, in his case. It is to speak the truth. That, to this hour, he has defiantly refused to do. Worse, he has spent much time and contrivance to undo the truth.

If this were a matter touching only him and me, it might be of little moment. Obviously, it goes far beyond any individual man. We are not playing games; we are dealing with the lives of "children's children" in the world we are preparing for them. There are insurrectionists of the 1956 revolt, sitting in Hungarian jails, and in the night that falls when hope fails absolutely, whose fate is touched by Hiss' defiance. And I find it difficult in the extreme to understand how certain of his perfervid partisans can pay lip-service to those resisters and their cause, and not make the basic equation between his defiance and their suffering. Beside it, his own, however immeasurable, loses scale. "With every dawn," Camus tells us of our time, "masked assassins slip into some cell; murder is the question before us." An historic lie on this scale helps turn the key that lets the murderers in.

A Central Lesion

But we do not need to travel so far as Budapest. That celebrated defiance touches much closer home. It divides the minds of some of the best men and women among us at a point on which, in this juncture of the human crisis, they need to be (and we need that they should be) most clear: the point of truth. Hiss' defiance perpetuates and keeps from healing a fracture in the community as a whole. And this is particularly true of that part of the community which is (or should be) the custodian and articulator of its collective virtue, *i.e.*, its mind. For when you accept a lie and call it truth, you have poisoned truth at the source, and everything else is sickened with a little of that poison. If you are looking for its monument, look around you.

You may say that all this is past and tiresome, try to sweep it largely out of sight and mind, and resolve briskly to get on to more pressing things. Your resolution remains chiefly bustle. The least, brushing touch (like this of Hiss' travels) shows that the wound is there, and fresh, and that its poisons continue to drain through the system. That is why the Hiss Case, though it has become modish in certain circles to glance away, though its dimensions in themselves are small among so many greater lesions, remains a central lesion of our time. That is why, ultimately, I cannot say (however differently I should prefer to get at it, at another level) that Alger Hiss has paid any effective penalty. For precisely he can end the lesion at any moment that he chooses, with half a dozen words.

Freedom to Travel

So much for that part of the direct quotation which I claim to be misquoted, and which, in any case, does not reflect my view. The rest of the quotation is fairly reported: "Alger Hiss is an American citizen. He has every right to apply for and receive a passport." This *does* reflect my view, though it was chiefly chance that it was said about Alger Hiss. I suspect that the misleading words were inserted (no doubt, with the best intention) by some newsman, trying to explain, for his own heart's ease, and his readers', how so bizarre a view came to be held by me.

The reason, if dismaying to some, is simpler than the one dreamed up. I am a bug on the question of unrestricted travel, as I am against the obscenities of wire-tapping, mail tampering, and related mischiefs that, in the name of good intention, are helping to pave the road that leads to 1984. I hold strongly that it is a right of man and of the citizen to travel freely where and when he will, and that any extensive restriction of that right is among the usurpations that feed the Total State. Of course, I know the arguments from expediency; here security is "the question before us." I have seen scarcely a shred of evidence, by contrast with the many sweeping arguments, that convinces me on this score. It is not the known Communists whose travels need greatly alarm us. Let them travel where they will, and let us observe their travels. They will take us to their leader, and possibly many NCO's en route. A dozen secret services, not only ours, must exist to watch them. It is the unknown Communist (or sympathizer) whose travels may work us harm; and to him a passport would be issued without question, in any case, because we do not know who or what he is.

So strong has this argument from expediency (or fear)

become, that we have all but forgotten how recent travel restriction is. My generation grew up in an almost passportless world. In those days, the Russian Autocracy and the Turkish Sultanate were considered semi-barbarous, in part because almost alone, they inflicted on their nationals the uncivilized indignity of passports. To me travel restriction seems chiefly to multiply the files behind which bureaucracies always gratefully barricade and entrench their positions, and fiercely defend them.

No doubt, in some quarters on the Right, such views will put me in a lonely minority. I can only urge most careful reflection on the matter. A little shift in the political weather, and it may be the spokesmen of the Right whose freedom of travel is restricted— with a certain smugness. The grounds will be expediency, of course. The precedent will be almost unassailable. Anti-Communists will have promoted it.

I think I can hear a crescent rumble rising: "Why, the man is talking like a Liberal." I have scarcely any interest in invective tags. My concern is not for the political geography of this or that position, but whether or not the position taken makes sense, and is, to that degree, as we say: justified. And of course I know too: Woe to those who grope for reality, and any approximate truth that maybe generalized from it, in the No Man's Land between incensed camps. History and certain personal experiences leave me in little doubt about the fate of such seekers. They are fair game to the snipers of both sides, and it is always open season. But while Mr. Hiss hurries to his plane or ship, and the snipers wait for the man to reach, in his groping, the point where the hairlines cross on their sights, I may still have time to sort the dead cats into tidy piles—those from one camp, here; those from the other, there. As one of my great contemporaries put it: "Anybody looking for a quiet life has picked the wrong century to be born in." The remark must be allowed a certain authority, I think, since the century clinched the point by mauling with an axe the brain that framed it.

June 20, 1959

Foot in the Door

The googols are coming, and against them the College Door is Closing. A student who has Done It Himself suggests: Put Aeschylus in orbit

I t looks to me as if The George Washington University (in Washington, D.C.) were helping to pioneer something whose long-range implications may be pretty important for a lot of us. What it implies, if I am right about it, is the beginning of the breakthrough in mass education, by using television. Of course, other institutions have been experimenting with television education, and on a grander scale. But George Washington's project happens to be the one that I have seen close up; so I shall limit myself to it. The larger significance of this development seems scarcely possible to overrate. Among other mercies, if time and a fuller curriculum justify the general use of TV for teaching, that would seem to thrust a formidable foot into the Closing College Door.

By now, there cannot be many of us who are unfamiliar with that implacably Closing Door. Daily, and sometimes several times a day, it has been threatening to slam in our faces, or our children's or grandchildren's. The problem posed by the Closing College Door is due not only to our population explosion, but to the realization, abruptly brought home by those sky-writing Sputniks, etc., that: 1) a lot more Americans are going to have to be educated a lot better and more quickly than in the past; and that 2) henceforth education bears directly on national security and possibly national survival. On the TV screen, we see a flutter of black and white flakes, rather like snow mixed with soot. This is radioactive fallout; and, any day now, an accompanying voice tells us, we may find ourselves in the midst of it. The voice is unruffled, almost cosy—*nil desperandum Teucro duce et auspice Teucro*—as if you and I or the commentator were the kind of people who would ever let ourselves show surprise at a little radioactive fallout.

Behold the contrast with the Closing College Door. Nothing lulling about this one. The accompanying voice is that of the Education Lobby. The scene on the TV screen is full of pathos, too. We see Willie, gowned in his high school graduation togs, clutching his diploma, all set for the next step: going to College. Heartbreak: Willie isn't going anywhere, except that he is fated to go forever un-higher-educated. For—a Delphic voice warns us— by 1984 (or whatever the fateful deadline is) the Closing College Door will have slammed shut in Willie's eager face. Googols of secondary school graduates will be besieging the gates of campuses, quite futilely, since college facilities will be totally inadequate to cope with such hordes. (In case you do not yet realize what age you have been born into, a googol is shorthand for a digit followed by one hundred zeros.) We are invited to write for a leaflet, setting forth these matters more fully, from an address sufficiently pseudonymous to stir a surmise that this is an air-hole of the Education Lobby, or one of its isotopes.

Our Own Dollars

The problem of the Closing College Door is beyond question a real one. And it would be impermissible to treat Willie and his plight so lightly, if this particular presentation of it did not remind us uneasily of the commercials which try to persuade us that virility is inseparable from smoking certain brands of cigarettes. In each case, we resent a sneak assault on good sense. In Willie's case, it takes no great wits to guess what we are expected to do next: shake out what is left in our lank wallets while we pressure our legislators (themselves, paradoxically, not always beacons of literacy) to syphon federal taxes into higher education. Parents are not, apparently, presumed to be educated (or natively bright) enough to perceive that federal aid to education is their own tax-ravaged and inflated dollars fed into academic tills by other-directed and coercive means.

Perhaps it will come to this. But let us not delude ourselves about what it is we shall have come to. This is the age of euphemism, because this is the age of the Total State that is dawning, more or less everywhere, though under various softening and dissembling names and forms, on various impressive pretexts or necessities. But it is not deemed expedient that we should grasp what age it really is—at least, not all at once, or all of us at once. So, perhaps, of necessity, the State must soon be into the Business of Education, as the witty and bracingly arrogant Professor J. K. Galbraith assured us, only the other day, that it must.

. . . and Gladly Paid

But must it? It is just here that that formidable foot I mentioned may have got into the Closing College Door. Which brings us back to The George Washington University and its television project. Early this year, the University's College of Special Studies, in cooperation with Station WTOP (the *Washington Post*), offered a TV course in Russian for beginners. Within a fortnight or so, some 3,400 students had paid their fees (up to $75), and enrolled for the course. Perhaps it is worth remembering that Russian (like English) is one of the most difficult of the great cultural languages; and that, until recently, those who struggled with it had to rise before daybreak for the lectures which go on the air at 6:30 a.m. That invisibly listening 3,400 must form one of the biggest classrooms anywhere. They equal the entire population of many a college campus. Bear in mind, too, that they are being taught by a single instructor—the very competent Mr. Vladimir Tolstoy. One mind efficiently instructing a formally enrolled class of 3,400 other minds—it is at that point that the possibilities of television education begin to open out. When this is possible and comparatively simple, why need the Closing College Door close, or be held open chiefly by the strong-arm State? Why cannot a comparatively small faculty (and a highly select one at that) instruct millions just as well as 3,400?

The Education Lobby

I am not an educator, so that the reasons why not do not leap to my mind as fleetly as I have no doubt they will leap to authoritative minds. Some of the objections must certainly be well taken, if only on grounds of ca' canny. Some, we may feel reasonably sure, will be simple obstruction, not perhaps consciously identified as such by the obstructors. For here we run up against the rooted human reluctance to innovation (a reluctance for which, at times, there is something to be said), but which, perhaps rather more often, amounts to a dense inertia. We also get into the preserves of vested academic interest. And I incline to the view that Fafnir, grunting and belching over the Niebelung Hoard, was a tame and temperate dragon compared to schoolmen, guarding academic interests to which they have staked claims during dedicated lifetimes, with little enough recognition, and few of this world's rewards.

Here, too, we can only brush the powerful forces, which we lump loosely as the Education Lobby, and which appear, in general, to be bound by the most tender, consanguine ties to vaster, more powerful forces that look to the State as the sovereign solvent of our social (and most other) problems. And this, not because such heads are peculiarly mischievous, wicked or (as an otherwise intelligent Conservative said to me recently) "immoral." Mischief and malignity might be comparatively easy to deal with. But these folk are, in general, intelligent, articulate, and intellectually effective, to the degree in which, having looked into the problem and sounded its complexities in depth, they find no agency but the State adequate to solving it on such a scale. It is this, precisely, that gives them a quite unbearable moral presumption. They also note that, given the general pattern of the age, the whole momentum of historical forces, quite apart from what anybody might want to do, or not to do, about it, is working to strengthen the State. And their sense of riding this irresistible momentum is precisely what gives them an insufferable self-righteousness. Since anything that magnifies the power of the State hastens a process, which is deemed inevitable, whatever tends to speed it up shortens it, and is, to that degree, beneficent. Anything that slows it down is unintelligent, maleficent, and, in such terms, "immoral." That is to say, much the same judgment reached by my Conservative friend, but reached from the other direction by reading the same terms in a reverse sense.

Since the Closing College Door tends to strengthen the State, that Door is a godsend to such folk, and they may be expected to put their full and ululant weight behind it, and against anything that might keep it ajar. They do not necessarily think of it this way. But we are not speaking here about what individual heads think, but about relationships of forces and interests, and what happens when individual men are drawn by them into action, which has a way of depersonalizing most of us. In any event, if televised education really threatens to thrust a foot in the Closing College Door, we may well see some plain and fancy surgery to sever the foot at the ankle.

Lines of Attack

One line of surgery seems obvious. While talking with the head of the Slavic Department and others at George Washington, I thought I caught the whine of the whetstone just behind their backs. The same sound seemed phrased in a question on the form that many TV students filled out for the College of Special Studies: "Can Education be successfully given over TV?" My answer: "No question whatever about it; it can."

Another line of attack is easily foreseen. Presumably, it would go much like this. Suppose you are televising not just a single course; and one, too, about which there is, admittedly, a touch of fad. Suppose you are televising a full semester's high school or college work, especially to younger students. When they are put on their own, largely removed from the hourly discipline of class attendance and supervision, what grounds have you for expecting, what right have you to expect, that the mass of such students would do the necessary work? My reaction to that one is brief, blunt, and to many, I should think, abhorrent: about this the Russians seem to me unquestionably right. Those who cannot learn should be spared the ordeal. Those who will not learn should be spared the privilege. If they will not learn, and, while learning, keep to a certain standard of progress—into the factories with them, or stores, or any occupation that will usefully employ (and train) their hands and heads, without making undue demands upon their minds. At the same time, every effort should be made to help out of routine, stultifying jobs young (and older) people who can, and *will*, use their minds, but are prevented from learning by the need to earn. No use to say that this is undemocratic. This selective process, and only this one, is truly democratic, drawing out of the fecund, unranked body of the nation, the forces on which, when trained, depends the well-being of the community as a whole.

In the past, our slackness about learning did not matter. At least, it did not matter enough to justify so drastic a stand. But the past and its easy ways (which I, personally, prefer to anything that is likely to take their place) helps us little or nothing now. We are visibly on a historical turning-point which is all but certain to determine the human condition for an unforeseeable reach of time. How that turning-point comes out for us, turns, in a much more foreseeable degree, on what the oncoming generations make of their minds. And not only the oncoming generations. There are plenty of adult minds (a sizable arsenal of them, one suspects) whose efficiency a little easily accessible education would greatly step up, probably to their own considerable exhilaration.

TV Screen and Campus

I am not suggesting, of course, that televised education can replace (or displace) Harvard—letting that name stand, *in excelsis*, for many others. No merely functional teaching is likely to be a substitute for a campus education with its celebrated intangibles, dedicated to shaping, as we are reminded at almost any Commencement exercises, "the whole man." There is also a fairly dreary waste (which also has its justifying arguments) in any college education. Ninety windows smashed in one fraternity house in one glorious night (to cite an item of rather recent personal recollection) scarcely seem indispensable to shaping "the whole man." Nor is all the waste on the side of the students, as anybody knows who has been exposed to the enshrined prejudices, posturings and crotchets of certain old faculty boys of nostalgic memory. These, too, have their justifications, though one cannot help wondering how those antics might go over on a TV screen under the sobering stare of millions.

I am not suggesting, either, that televised education is coming tomorrow, or that it does not pose its own order of grave and complex problems; or that it is a cure-all for our educational plight. I am saying only that the need is great, pressing, and generally conceded; that, in television, a means to meet the need, at least in part, appears to be at hand; that it is comparatively inexpensive and need not involve the State. What is required next would seem to be the will to mate the means and the need; to work out organizational and other problems, which, however difficult, are likely to be somewhat less so than those of splitting the atom or orbiting a rocket around the sun. I venture that, if need and means were brought together, the public response might be at least as startling as the response to The George Washington University's Russian course.

In fact, the problem's thrust outstrips all such terms. It is clear that mankind may, within a rather short time, blow itself into a poisonous powder and lie dusting a vaster putrefaction. I happen to believe that the odds, though touch and go, are rather against apocalypse. If this proves true, it seems to me that, for a century or so, the energies of mankind will be increasingly directed to, and absorbed, with an exclusive and unparalleled intensity, in raising the level of human material well-being, *i.e.*, social wealth, and in solving certain related problems. One of the beneficent side-effects of the crisis of the twentieth century as a whole, is a dawning realization, not so much that the mass of mankind is degradingly poor, as that there will be no peace for the islands of relative plenty until the continents of proliferating poverty have been lifted to something like the general material level of the islanders. It is this perfectly practical challenge, abetted by a sound self-interest, which must engross the energies of mankind, and more and more, perhaps, inspire it as a perfectly realizable vision. Especially, I should think, it would inspire Americans, who, in a sense, invented abundance; and who appear to feel what other nations have felt as a sense of destiny, only in the generous act of bringing their abundance, and the know-how behind it, to less fortunate breeds.

But the world is also degradingly ignorant—and by no means only in Africa. Unless the general level of mind is raised at the same time as the level of material well-being, and not too many steps behind, we shall all risk resembling those savages whom, within living memory, civilizers introduced to the splendor of top hats and tight shoes, for the greater glory of their extremities, leaving unredeemed the loin-cloth of their middle zones, and the wits between their ears.

In the Next Century

In fact, we shall have little choice but to raise the level. A modern economy of abundance cannot be sustained, cannot even be organized, without also organizing (*i.e.*, educating) the brains to run it. At the point where such brains must number millions, education must almost certainly take to the air. It seems extremely doubtful that the old local centers of learning, however expanded, can cope with twenty-first century needs. They will doubtless long retain their glory, which will draw to them the élite of the élite for the refinement of knowledge. But the educational scale of the future would seem to require solutions in something approaching googol terms.

Still, men are incurably traditional, no doubt because they are irremediably mortal—a circumstance that no amount of material wellbeing is likely to change much. So every revolution prepares a conservatism of new forms. Patterns of convention, symbol, ritual reassert themselves to provide a comfort and a reassuring hand-hold on the slowly sinking ship, which, since each of us always dies, each of us always is. So perhaps, when the great television universities of the future go on the air, beaming their courses from satellite stations orbited in space, students in Katmandu or Cochabamba, before tuning in, may bow three times ceremoniously toward Cambridge (U.K. or Mass.) and the University of California at Los Angeles, though they may no longer know or care just why they make this ritual gesture. Only the oldest old boys may mumble, between their stainless steel teeth, of a legend that, in the centuries BTE (Before Television Education), Oxford, Princeton, Yale, and the like, were names for high places of the mind by which the wonder came.

Remembering Chambers

The following articles appeared in the
July 29, 1961 issue of National Review

Il Faut le Supposer Heureux

The following is from the last letter I received from
Whittaker Chambers.

—William F. Buckley Jr.

Pipe Creek Fann
Westminster, Md.
April 9, 1961

Dear Bill,

. . . Weariness, Bill—you cannot yet know literally what it means. I wish no time would come when you do know, but the balance of experience is against it. One day, long hence, you will know true weariness and will say: "That was it." My own life of late has been full of such realizations: "So that was why he did that"; "So that was why she didn't do that"; about the past acts of people with whom my own age (and hence understanding) has only just caught up. There's a kind of pathos about it—a rather empty kind, I'm afraid; the understanding comes too late to do even the tardy understander much good.

Our kind of weariness. History hit us with a freight train. History has long been doing this to people, monotonously and usually lethally. But we (my general breed) tried, as Strachey noted, to put ourselves together again. Since this meant outwitting dismemberment, as well as resynthesizing a new life-view (grandfather, what big words you use), the sequel might seem rather remarkable, rather more remarkable than what went before. But at a price—weariness. People tend to leave Oedipus, shrieking with the blood running down his cheeks—everybody nicely purged by pity and terror, and so home and to bed. But I was about 23 when I discovered, rather by chance, that Oedipus went on to Colonnus. But each of us, according to his lights, was arrested in time by the same line—the one in which Oedipus, looking out from precarious sanctuary after long flight, sums up: "Because of my great age, and the nobility of my mind, I feel that all will be well." That is the Oedipus largely overlooked. Of course, I can say nothing of the nobility of my mind, or even Koestler's or Camus'; and I realize, too, that Oedipus spoke at a grateful moment of rescue. One cannot pretend to live at that height. And yet, to reach it even at times is something. One must have got rid of great loads of encumbering nonsense and irrelevance to get there; must have learned to travel quite light—one razor, one change, etc. And I suppose the "well" of the quotation is almost wholly a subjective value. And there remains the price—the weariness I mentioned which none of us complains about, but should take good care not to inflict on other people's lives. I did and I'm sorry about it. We're grateful too.

Something quite different which struck me—what seems to have been your desolation by *Man's Fate* [by André Malraux]. But Hemmelrich goes back (supreme tenderness) to close the door left too hastily open on the bodies of his murdered wife and son. Tchen, about to throw himself and bomb under the automobile, believes that Pei (spared to life because Tchen acts alone) will be able to write more meaningfully by reason of Tchen's act. Kyo takes the cyanide with the sense that the concept of man's dignity enjoins control over his own death. Katow, surrendering even that ultimate, divides his cyanide with those less able to bear man's fate; and walks toward the locomotive through a hall of bodies from which comes something like an unutterable sob—the strangled cry. It may also be phrased: "And the Morning Stars sang together for joy." It may also be phrased: *"Il faut supposer Katow heureux,"* as Camus wrote: *"Il faut supposer Sisyphe heureux."* For each age finds its own language for an eternal meaning.

As always,

Whittaker

Wisdom Is the Most Terrible Ordeal

By Duncan Norton-Taylor

We always brought away more than we could take them on our visits to the Maryland farm: the stimulation of his ideas and his insight into history, which always brought an ordinary journalist up short; his mysterious humor, his profound pessimism which, curiously, left a sense of the stature not the meanness of man; we would also drive off with some of Esther's preserves, and plants to put in our garden—we brought away so much of their affection. The conversations didn't just touch on men and the world. We also talked about children and growing up and such matters, calves, lambs, which fascinated Whittaker.

I have a letter from him dated March 1, 1951: "After several days of warm fine weather we had cold and sleet last night, so Willett's Lillian, having carefully watched the weather, decided to lamb. Esther found the shivering lamb early this morning. Willett's Lillian is the grand champion of Maryland. Therefore she would have to have her lamb on the coldest day, and to have the weakest lamb. I have been working over it for an hour or so, filling it with warm milk and Haig & Haig. I've rigged it an incubator on the gas stove. It has got over its drunk and is now warm, sassy and baaing like an Ingersoll watch being wound. It is also doing its best to upset the incubator. Lots of trouble. . . ."

That was before the first coronary thrombosis, on Election night, 1952, that exiled him from the barns and separated him from his lambs, and denied him for a long while his walks along the creek that runs through Pipe Creek Farm. But the world wouldn't even let him alone in bed. Only his wife knows of all the people with their conspirings and cross-purposes and axes to grind who came through the farmhouse door—the door that was forced open by the Hiss case and never could be closed again. He wrote shakily early in March of 1953, lying on his back, "Do you remember saying to me, 'There will never be an end to it, will there?' I am afraid only one. The man simply drops off the piece of wreckage because his fingers get numb, and his will." I could only reply that I thought he still had a pretty fair grip, which as it turned out he did. A fair grip.

What recollections do you have of a friend who is dead? A man in a chair across the room. His chuckle that is more seen than heard, when one of his sudden, secret jokes lights his face and shakes his stomach (which he knows is much too big for a man with a bad heart although this doesn't worry him too much). His voice gently chiding Esther for rushing around the way she does, trying to wait on him and everyone else all at once. His voice becoming somber and sometimes so low as to be almost inaudible, but never lifted in outrage even at the motley legion that attacked him (still attacks him). He never avowed any special quality of forgiveness, but he had an understanding of man that was close to forgiveness. You recollect a stout figure unexpectedly arrayed in a brand new suit trying to appear the sophisticated traveler, when the two of them are off for Europe—and Esther almost speechless with excitement over her first trip abroad. On an earlier occasion, when it was we who were going to Europe, he wrote, "Come back soon. We shall feel your absence as an empty space."

Now the shoe is permanently on the other foot.

There can be the recollection of a mourned friend's words to help fill the empty space. There are his letters over the years. Some of them included fragments, I am sure, of the thoughts he was projecting into a book. He never finished the book—or books, for at one point the project had grown in his mind into two books that would make, with *Witness*, a trilogy. One difficulty was that, although he described the main stream with tremendous clarity, he was so much of a journalist himself that the sudden odd twists of events kept engaging his attention and distracting him. He also felt the book was his last testament, which was a fearful (and foolish) psychological burden to assume. At any rate the project was never completed and I cannot console myself.

As I say, we often talked in the kitchen about children. One day in June, which for children is the month of endings and beginnings, he wrote: "They will always, if they are worth anything at all, head for the stairway down to sea ('Down which the blind are driven'). We, if we are worth anything at all, will always tell them about the roaring of the sea, its drowning depth. It will do little good. But in the end, if they and we live long enough, they will revere us to the degree in which they do not have to absolve us of our pity. For what they need from us is not pity, but wisdom. And it is only after they have grievously earned wisdom themselves that they will understand fully that, while pity is childish, wisdom is the most terrible ordeal that men can suffer or practice. Among the oddments which clutter my mind is one about an old Chinese who sank down, down, down in life until in the world's eyes he was nothing. The final stroke for him was that his daughter went into the Concessions and was Westernized. That was her ordeal. And how well she understood hers and his, and their meaning each to each can be caught in the fact that each letter she wrote him in his poverty until he died began: 'Honored Great Father.'"

I have spoken of pessimism. "Your pessimism may well outsweep my own," he once remarked, I think with some amusement. Exactly what prompted it I do not now remember, but there was a long letter in April 1955. I think we may have gotten into a theological discussion, because he wrote in part: "Every system founders on the unknowable and the tragic. Each leaves us at last, as if we had never troubled to stir, on our knees before that Cross and within the sound of those mortal words, 'My God, My God, why has Thou forsaken me?'—which are, moreover, the irreducible starting point of faith—they, and not: 'God is love.'"

Then he went on: "Not long ago, as I may have told you, I found myself talking with a former member of the Politburo of the German Communist Party. At the end of a long and instantly intimate talk, in which we found ourselves at one about the meaning of most of what was happening to us all, he asked me suddenly: 'Is there no hope?' I said: 'There is no hope.' He said in a low voice: 'I tremble in the night.' I saw that he had not understood me and that, by his nature, he never could understand me. But I thought I must try to explain, if only, as we say, for the record. I said: 'You tremble in the night because you are looking for hope in the wrong place. There are no *political* solutions left. There are only martyrdoms. But martyrdom does not speak primarily to the present. It speaks to the future and to posterity.' He said: 'Then I'm at the end of my Latin [for me school is out].' That is why I wrote to a friend who had listened to the conversation: 'Bobbi, who disdains all dialectic, cannot therefore divine the deepest dialectic of all. Hence he cannot understand that, in that dialectic, hope must always pace despair which always goes a little ahead. And he cannot glimpse the degree to which despair itself is the force that moves hope to equal it in order to outmatch it—or the degree to which, in that process, hope must come to resemble despair.

" 'Bobbi's hope is still a little child, which has learned only to read the news reports of strategies and the statistics of steel production. That is why he said, 'Whittaker has lost hope.' Because he cannot see how Maria (the Maria of *Witness*), a slave in a padded jacket and lapti, staring hopelessly through the barbed wire of Vorkuta, may be more the hope of the world than all the intercontinental ballistic missiles in the stockpile. He cannot discern through her rags that most dog-eared truth: the light shines in darkness.'"

From a Letter, December 1959

Whittaker Chambers

I f you re-read *Darkness at Noon* at this late hour you will see how true it is a book of poetry. I re-read it recently. I came to the part where, after his breakdown, Rubashov is permitted a few minutes of air in the prison yard. Beside him trots the Central Asian peasant who has been jailed because, "at the pricking of the children," the peasant and his wife had barricaded themselves in their house and "unmasked themselves as reactionaries." Looking sideways at Rubashov in his sly peasant way, he says: "I do not think they have left much of Your Honor and me." Then, in the snow of the prison yard and under the machine-gun towers, he remembers how it was when the snow melted in the mountains of Asia, and flowed in torrents. Then they drove the sheep into the hills, rivers of them, "so many that Your Honor could not count them all." I cannot go on reading because I can no longer see the words. To think that any man of my time could have written anything so heart-tearingly beautiful, "wonderful, causing tears." This is what makes K so precious to me. This pure creativity which is more than, by taking thought, he could evoke: *O fons Bandusiae, splendidior vitre.*

Let Only a Few Speak for Him

By Ralph de Toledano

S ome men are touched by God, and in turn they reach out to others the grace of their intuition. Such a man was Whittaker Chambers. Only the foolish and the mediocre denigrated him. For evil in its own way recognizes and respects the good, however it may hate. Now he is dead, out of the mind's reach, a solitary figure in the history he knew so well and helped to make. Those of us who knew him, who shared his trust or had a sometime view of the life he saw through those laughing, prescient eyes, can reread his letters and weep and know the cold edge of our loss. Why write of him when he has so much better written of himself? Why beat hopelessly at a door that is locked and adamant in its exclusion?

There is a reason. Whittaker Chambers was my friend, my father, my brother—and sometimes my son. But this is my private concern. A public duty resides in those who remain, transitory between eternities, to speak of the dead. We do not honor them, but ourselves. And if we utter our longing and sorrow, it is a prayer to the God who made us and who will judge us at the End Day. We also make our witness before a hostile world. He knew what that hostility would be. Writing to me on Easter Sunday 1956, his fifty-fifth birthday, Whittaker Chambers said: "I hope you have my obit ready. What fun the yappy little dogs will have. I don't even begrudge it them, rest seems so welcome."

Through all the years that I knew him—the terrible time of the trial, the time of pain after the first heart attack, the time when he was forced by ill-health to absent himself from the felicity of the soil he loved so dearly—it was rest he wanted. This was something that his own nature could not give him. The desire for rest was always in conflict with an abounding sense of life. In the beautiful "back farm" to which he withdrew, he could look down a long vista in the summer quiet. He could wake early to hear the clamor of the birds, or step outside his door to feed the wild animals that did not fear his presence. But he surveyed far more than the pond and the trees and the far-away mountains. Sitting with friends on the small porch, his speech was rich in literary and historical allusion, all interwoven and all relating to the final conflict in which Christian civilization finds itself. The French Revolution, the marching sailors of Kronstadt, the death of the monarchic principle in England at the hands of Cromwellian mobs—these were all as vividly alive to him as the fighters in Budapest or his life in the Communist underground.

In a very precise way, he always saw himself in the past and in perspective. Writing to me and of me, yet really of himself, he could say: *"A man's special truth is in the end all there is in him. And with that he must be content though life give him no more, though man give him nothing. Must be content, that is, unless it comes upon him that wisdom itself is the ultimate folly, the ultimate presumption. I am myself so much in the sunset that all things cast their shadows eastward from me."*

He knew that he had made his witness, that he had stood before God stripped of pretension, humble yet unashamed. He had seen the Behemoth and never flinched, except for one despairing moment when death had seemed the single answer to a world gone so neurotic that it had forgotten the only pride not offensive to God: the pride of the man who is ready to fight and die for what he knows to be right and true. He was a symbol of that pride, and he had the intellectual courage to set his own worth high. Yet he knew that his witness might have been in vain, much like that of the Christian in the arena who felt the gladiator's sword pierce his flesh and felt the warm, red blood covering his loins.

After Alger Hiss had been convicted, when the yawping press expected exultation, he could write: *"The days that will diminish the echoes of the trial already reveal that I have an all but incurable wound. My good, intuitive friend, Marjorie Kinnan Rawlings, wrote during the first trials 'When this is over, I believe that you are planning to kill yourself.' In the literal sense, this was not true, but it was so close to my feeling from the beginning that I have never trusted myself to answer her. At the end of that day of turmoil in which I decided to put the Baltimore [espionage] papers in evidence, I thought 'Because of Esther and the children, I cannot pray to God to let me die, but I cannot keep from hoping that He will.' Now this feeling dogs me through these beautiful, unseasonable days and in the hours of the night when I wake. There keep running through my head two epitaphs that Byron saw in an Italian graveyard:* 'implora eterna pace,' 'implora eterna quieta.' *'All they ask for is peace,' Byron noted. 'And that they implore.'*

"Add to this the feeling that it was all for nothing, that nothing has been gained except the misery of others, that it was a tale of the end and not of the beginning of something. . . . You cannot save what cannot save itself. These things happened because our sector of the world could not understand what was happening to it. It does not understand yet, nor does it understand this Case."

This was the theme that ran through everything he said or wrote. This was the cause of his impatience at many anti-Communists who saw the final conflict solely in terms of counter-espionage, of disclosure, of military maneuvering. The battle was one of faith—and as the Crusades demonstrated, such wars were fought in grime and terror unknown to the tea-party pundits whose vocation was splitting hairs and making self-defeating distinctions. When a lady writer for one of the more rarified "little" magazines went through her exercises on the Case, Whittaker Chambers was at once amused and indignant. He was too charitable to assail her in print, to note her tardy record of recognition, but in the privacy of his correspondence, he cut close to the heart of the matter. *"The Chambers attitude, as he has said, is based on respect of a common power to hold faith, at an intensity and with a force, that the xxxxxx's do not know or admit. Is it nice? Is dirt nice? Is death nice? Above all, is dying nice? And, in the end, we must ask: Is God nice? I doubt it.*

Der Gott der Eisen waohsen liess,
Er wollte keine Knechte.

"And since you refuse to know German, I translate:

The God who made iron grow—
He wanted no slaves.

"The world in which you and I exist and bow our heads before the God who made it, is the world also of the atom bomb and virus. The mystery lies beyond the lady's cerebration—or in yours or mine. But if the neat, efficient, competent brain denies or by-passes the mystery? That is the point whose bended edge divides men into breeds between which mind may be an extenuator or a compromiser, but cannot change or assimilate the breeds. And the breed of Hiss will always be nearer to the breed of Chambers than it can ever be to the breed of xxxxxx. Because the first two contain the power to hold faith; the second admits only to the ability to entertain reason and a reasoned viewpoint."

Whittaker Chambers was always a man of faith, and it was this which kindled the love of millions who know that transcendental hunger. As a very young man he saw what war and starvation had done to a defeated Germany. He saw what depression could do in a confident United States. And having been educated and trained in that citadel of materialism, Columbia College, he thought he discovered the antidote to these poisons in Communism. The tentative and the wishful were not for him, and he gave everything to the solution which fitted his comprehension. He might have been as great and productive a writer as this country had ever known, but he tossed aside his personal ambitions in a cause he believed was just. The polite Communism of the intellectuals who hung their clothes on the hickory limb but never went near the water was not for him. He plunged into the real business of Communism—and only the grace of God prevented you and me from doing the same. But it was in his nature to realize that faith is but part of a trinity—that it is also incumbent of hope and love, the hope which is part of the human condition and the *caritas* which Christ at Golgotha gave us. And so, in fear and determination, he broke with Communism.

I began to know Whittaker Chambers in the early days of the Case—when the press with almost homosexual love was fawning over Alger Hiss, but lying in wait to pound Chambers with scatological questions. When I face my God, I will be confronted with many sins, but I will be able to say: In the hours of his sorrow, I stood by him and could give him friendship and love. It was a small thing—and repaid a millionfold with the gift of understanding. Of this there will be no more, for it would be obscene to clothe myself in his greatness. It is all there in his letters, in the poems he allowed me to see—but they are for my private comfort. God so loved the world that He gave His only begotten Son—and in my personal grief I can only say that without blaspheming, I know, I really know.

Whittaker Chambers is dead. For him there is rest. For us, there are only the simple words, *ora pro nobis*. In another age and another time, he would have stood by the seats of the mighty and guided their hands. In these times, he guided me through the thicket to the open plain where the light of God shines through—understanding of my weaknesses, but forgiving. And what can I offer in requiem? Let him speak in poems he wrote, imperfect but dear, and never shown to cruel eyes.

The bird sings,
releasing as it flies
the umbel of a flower that swings,
unimplicated, over stones
where the blood already dries
in fluffs of fur;
while expeditious emmets stir,
triggered mystically to feed,
before flies breed
maggots to compete.

And again:

All things work together for good,
as every field
of springing grain
is dunged with filth and death,
and rots the falling rain
which double duty dies,
multiplying yield,
and simulating peace;
which is always for the ear
that cannot hear;
for the eye that is blind,
or set behind;
is always for the ending,
never for the beginning, breath

Is the web where hangs
the suavely packaged fly
that for only meaning has
a little sizzling cry,
whereby,
confides to capable arachnid

the monotony of the agony
of its plea to die
at once; and at the same time not to die. . . .

Others can rehearse the facts and the events that made up the life of Whittaker Chambers. Others can weep more eloquently than I for a man who knew the fate incumbent in the bone. For myself—for those who love freedom and who have been reached by his greatness—only this is valid: He died a martyr. Let us say our goodbyes. Now we must avenge him.

Death Deceived

Reprinted from the July 12, 1961 edition of
the Richmond News Leader

W hittaker Chambers died Sunday, but no one knew better than he that his life ended over a decade ago, on the witness stand. He was one of those men whose whole life is summed up and tested, under a cruel glare, in a single public act. He had lived the central experience of our time, and he had the courage to lay bare the heartbreaking emptiness of that experience. He destroyed himself in an agony of rendering up the truth about the modern world's great dreams of social reform and political utopia. His one great act, like Samson's, brought the pillars of an entire temple crashing down on him. Wise still, and witty to the end, with an imp of humor ever alive in him, he had nonetheless lived in a shell these last years. His life had already been poured out for others, in warning and witness.

Chambers bore witness against an age, against his friend, against himself. The cruel deception of Communism robbed the world for years of his eloquence and wisdom. In him, the hidden tragedy of Communism came to the surface—the grinding use of pity to enforce terror, the appeal to the human heart made by the very enemy of humanity. Chambers had lived with this tragedy, himself unbroken as he saw his fondest dreams break around him, watched his friends become weirdly distorted shapes in the nightmare world of dissemblance. He summoned the sheer nerve needed to renounce that dream, to reveal its lying center. He rose up to indict a dream, perfectly aware that those who are fond of dreaming would not hear. He called the wasted years before the bench, the twisted talents of a whole era, the fond pursuit of that giant joke on the human heart, Communism. He turned upon it, knowing its force, knowing that its time of defeat had not yet come, that the tide had not turned. He was not a conqueror, no opportunist deserting a lost cause. He was a witness.

That pointed finger, leveled at his friend, electrified our age and will haunt our history. It revealed, like a stab of lightning, this century's underworld of lost hopes and breeding terrors. And the life that ended in such a moment of truth will never end. Tricked by life, he succeeded in tricking death, Sunday's victory was deceptive; when death called, he had already gone. But while we live, and until the eclipse of the West, this figure stands central and alive, living still his death of demonstration; bearing witness.